VIEW FROM THE PIER
STORIES FROM SAN CLEMENTE

WRITTEN & ILLUSTRATED
BY HERMAN SILLAS

WPR BOOKS
CARLSBAD, CA

Cover Painting—View from the Pier—*This is a self-portrait of me standing on the San Clemente Pier looking out at Dana Point doing what I do best . . . nothing.*

Back cover photos by Gary Zuercher.

For more about books presented by WPR Publishing, please go to www.WPRbooks.com.

WPR BOOKS
3445 Catalina Dr., Carlsbad, CA 92010-2856
www.WPRbooks.com   760-434-1223   kirk@whisler.com

DEDICATION

I thank all those who have encouraged me to compile this book, especially Cora, my wife, who has always encouraged me to pursue my dreams and remained my greatest supporter and critic.

A special thanks to the San Clemente Sun Post News and the Hispanic Link Syndication for the opportunity to express my opinions in print. I have a deep appreciation for Gary Zuercher, my photographer who always makes his photos of my paintings seem like originals. I also wish to thank Chris Nesbitt, my son-in-law, for causing his camera to render me presentable. A special thanks to Susan Goetz who edited my manuscript and to Kirk Whisler, my publisher, for all of his encouragement and guidance.

This book is in honor of my parents, Herman and Lupe Sillas, who sacrificed to make sure that their children not only had a home, food and clothing, but also the opportunity to pursue the gifts that God gave us. Our parents' love was unending.

I dedicate this book to all those that walk the pier and enjoy its special charm. I believe the walk will make them all return to the shore wiser than when they left, because the pier is not just a wooden walkway above the waves, it is a pathway to inspiration.

TABLE OF CONTENTS

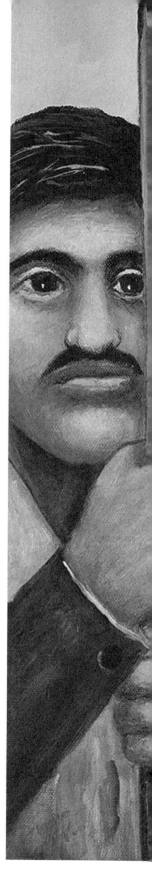

WHAT PEOPLE ARE SAYING ABOUT THE BOOK

"I always look forward to Herman Sillas' latest View FromThe Pier, because I know I'll learn something new. I'll get an inside view of the Mexican American struggle for civil rights, or a peek at life in a surfside community with all its characters and idiosyncrasies. I'll spend time with a loving couple and their family, or get a unique spin on the way our country operates. But what I love most is the way Herman paints the picture with great soul and a vibrant spirit, whether in words or on a canvas."

Liz Zuercher, writer, San Clemente, CA

"In this world of ours, at one time or another we will experience the good in life as well as the difficult. As I read and viewed Herman's stories, it didn't take long before I found myself in one of them ... just like you will. There is nothing more important than family, health, and friends as Herman so impressively articulates. Don't read these stories once, read them twice. Caramba!"

Reuben Martinez, Libraria Martinez de Chapman University

"I've enjoyed Mr. Sillas's writings and paintings for years. His writings are entertaining humorous and always sagacious. His paintings are symbolic of his cultural background and penetrating to the core of one's self identity."

Alex Jacinto, Los Angeles attorney

"To Herman Sillas, the San Clemente pier spans the edge of where massive land ends and the expansive ocean begins. It represents a special breath of life, an escape from problems, a oneness with nature, and a chance to clear out your mind and fill your lungs with sea air. His skillful narrative provides a mental conversation between the writer and the reader as each "view from the pier" evolves. His impressions of life as they have passed or are passing range from the silly and the sarcastic to the sensitive and serious. His mini-book is cleverly divided into six separate subject areas filled with the special observations of a writer/artist/lawyer/fisherman introduced by a relevant replica of his descriptive and colorful paintings. It's a must read. It's a cache of treasure."

Bill Thomas, college professor & feature writer

"I am proud to say that Herman's "FIESTA/USA" painting tops my private art collection, and I'm more than proud that he's a friend as well as an inspiration. He is the all-American story in the flesh, rising out of the old neighborhood in East L.A. to become a prominent attorney and then help so many others through his law firm. Both his work as an artist and writer reflect his admirable human touch and affection for life in every way. "

John Hall, retired Southern California news reporter and columnist

INTRODUCTION

I started fishing at the San Clemente Pier on weekends around 1988. I still remember the feeling I experienced the first morning I walked out with poles and tackle: freedom. My clients' legal problems stayed ashore; they didn't belong on the pier any more than fish did in a courtroom.

Something more than fishing calls me to the pier. Peace and solitude of the dawn are the drawing card, as light dances on water and highlights the spray from crashing waves. The sounds of seagulls as they take flight and the cooing of pigeons underneath the boardwalk fill my ears. From afar comes the barking of seals as they rest on their small rock island to the south. Before my eyes, colors change as the sun rises to warm a new day. The hues fascinate me as I scan the scene around me. It's a private moment with our Maker.

The pier pals begin arriving around seven. They walk the boardwalk daily and meet at the end of the pier for an exchange of news. On the way out they stop to inquire about my fishing luck. We chat and any topic becomes fair game.

I have grown to love San Clemente because of the pier pals, some of whom you will meet in the pages of this book. Besides pier pals, many others stroll the wooden quarter mile in the morning. I recognize that piers by their very existence extend an invitation to walk on water without getting wet. We all respond affirmatively.

San Clemente's pier is the symbol and energizer of the city. Take it away and this town is a different place. Just walk the pier's length or any part of it and you'll feel better. Walk it daily and you change the course of your life. No one complains about a pier stroll after returning to land. Lovers walk it slowly, runners faster, but thousands walk it every year. Why?

Is the answer the same one given by mountain climbers? "Because it's there." I think there's another reason.

Life looks different when you see it from the end of a pier standing over endless water. When you walk on the pier away from the beach, your view expands to include the coast. A bigger picture unfolds. It's the pier's perspective, a view from the pier.

Everyone needs a special thinking spot. We've had that need from the time we were small. As children we each had a special place where we could create our own world or think about what we were going to be when we grew up. As adults, the need still lingers.

I've heard people talking to themselves as they walk the pier, unconcerned that I, or anyone, heard them. A young fellow came out early one morning and danced and sang to music from his earphones. It never bothered me. I smiled because I understood he was doing his thing at his spot.

The San Clemente Pier is that spot for a lot of folks. I know it's mine. It's the breeding center for my stories. I have been very fortunate to have the San Clemente Sun Post News and the Hispanic Link Syndication share my "View from the Pier."

In preparing for the publication of this book, I reviewed my writings and found they fell into six categories. I didn't plan it that way; it just happened. I chose the ones that I thought would cause readers to think, laugh, maybe cry or make them feel good. No great wisdom is claimed in my efforts. They are thoughts that come where time is not a factor. As you read my stories you will notice that some were written many years ago, but hopefully the message is still relevant and will be enjoyed by you.

My paintings included in this book are of scenes that I saw on the pier or ones that reflect the themes of some of my stories.

Read in peace, because this book was put together with love from an old fisherman who loves this pier and the folks who enjoy it.

PART ONE: PIERS AND PALS

When I first started fishing at the San Clemente Pier early on weekend mornings, twenty-five years ago, I noticed a group of folks gathered at the shack near the end of the pier around 7:00 am. They engaged in conversation that was nonstop, but occasionally interrupted by laughter. By 8:30 am they had sauntered back to shore. I learned they met daily. I nicknamed them "pier pals" and in time I got to know many of them. Over the years some moved away or were no longer able to make the walk to the end of the pier. Others now stroll or fish on the big pier in the sky.

Still many are drawn to the pier like metal paper clips to a magnate. Some walkers I only know by sight. We acknowledge each other by a wave of a hand, a smile, or a head nod. Others stop to talk and I don't know their names. But I know John Lower, Jim Stevens, Nazareth (Naz) Horasanian, Marie Burke, Mariane Cook, Tom and Sue Bell, Barbara and Bob Baker, Don and Shirley Stanley, Steve and Vicky Carrico, Paul Gavin, Peg Homer, Paul and Cheryl Tyson, Andy Edward, and the two guys that run the pier shack and grill at the end of the pier, Randy Raneses and Eric Trevino. We are all pier addicts and have no desire to be cured.

Foggy Pier —*Mexican muralist Armando Campero and I ate breakfast at San Clemente's Fisherman's Restaurant one foggy morning. He said to me, "You ought to paint this fog." I did.*

EL NIÑO

When El Niño heralded its arrival with ten-foot waves and an appetite for the dry sand lying on our beaches, I and scores of San Clementians marched down to see if our beloved pier withstood the onslaught. It did. It also allowed us to walk out over the water for a quarter of a mile. Some talked of the pier's predecessor falling victim to Mother Nature in the past and were fearful it would happen again.

The waves were breaking beyond the pier and the surf rose high enough to scrub the underbelly of the extended boardwalk, wiping out the pigeon colony that had nestled there. The pigeons thought their nests and eggs would be safe from humans' and nature's interference but found there was no defense for El Niño. It came like an angry hombre.

Excitement saturated the beach air as we walked out on the pier that day. The wooden extension of the shore was like a finger in water testing the temperature, only this finger allowed us to test and feel the force of power that was being generated in the sea.

As I stood at the end rail of the pier facing the unstable horizon, the whitecaps breaking the surface of the darkened ocean gave evidence of the force that was being unleashed on our shores. The swaying floor I stood on, wet from the water spray, was a continual reminder of how vulnerable we are to the whims of nature.

I saw and felt the powerful waves reach up as far as they could, causing the flooring beneath me to move from side to side. Each wave brought comments from the assembly comparing one wave to another or speculating about the next one. We heard the power of the water as waves crashed into the moving surf beneath us. Sheets of dirty white water spray flew high into the air as if trying to escape the ultimate fate of every wave, regardless of its height, strength and power. They will all die on the sand of the beach that awaits their arrival. They remind me of ourselves, because we too have a date with a shore somewhere.

We watched the surfers who ventured out with their boards to try to ride El Niño's gift to them. I admired their courage and marveled at their skill as they balanced themselves on a wave's last moments of existence. At least there would be someone who would talk about a wave after its departure.

As I headed back to shore, I met parents and grandparents who brought children and tried to explain what was happening, while at the same time telling the little tots to hold on to the adult's hand, as if that would save anybody if Mother Nature decided to make this pier disappear like the Titanic. I saw old couples walking slowly together, reminiscing about more peaceful days and adding this stroll to what must be an already large volume of life.

The young strollers were boisterous as they interchanged "awesome" and "dude" in their conversations. Young men with girlfriends savored the moments when their female companions snuggled up to them indicating they were afraid of what they were witnessing and feeling. All of us were attempting to capture this moment in time. In the future we will be able to tell others of our stroll on the pier when El Niño arrived in San Clemente in 1998. Time will let us say that the waves were twenty feet high and that the pier swayed so much we almost fell off. All of that exaggeration is acceptable when you tell a story.

But when I was out there that afternoon, I couldn't help but think how important this pier is to this town. Without it, we would have been like many other beach town residents, standing on the shore looking at the waves and marveling at how high they were. But the pier provided an opportunity to venture out for a quarter of a mile and feel the force.

I'm glad I was there. I have a greater appreciation for this old wooden, weather-beaten boardwalk and those who made it. It brought a lot of people together that afternoon and allowed us to share an experience that we will long remember. I know I will as I stand out here fishing with a view from the pier.

TWO JOURNEYS

Fishing at dawn on the pier takes a special breed. We're like hermits without caves. Sometimes I'm there first. Other times this other guy beats me.

He first appeared about three years ago. We'd acknowledge each other's presence with a nod or a wave. That eventually evolved into "How's it going?" He stayed near the shore. I fished further out on the pier. Other than the greeting, we seldom talked. Fishermen are like that—respect for silence.

I eventually learned his name. He heard mine from the regulars who borrow my gaff to pull up mussels from the pilings. Then this guy asked if he could use it. He offered me bait from his efforts. I liked that about him.

Recently, we wound up fishing next to each other on a slow day. I became nosey. He is originally from Vietnam. When Saigon fell in 1975, he was a medium-ranked South Vietnamese government official.

The Communists put men like him in reeducation camps. He survived in the jungle swamp where prisoners had to grow their own food and build their quarters from whatever they could find. After two hard years, the Communists released him.

Still, they required him to report his daily activities weekly to the local police. His two attempts to escape Vietnam had been thwarted, but officials weren't aware of his efforts. Finally, in 1980, he and nineteen others escaped on a twenty-foot fishing boat at night. He paid $1,000 to the fisherman who owned the launch.

After three days and four nights the refugees' water and food were depleted. Fortunately, they were picked up by a Norwegian ship and taken to Norway. He had left his parents, four sisters and an older brother when he took the leap to freedom.

Landing in Oslo, Norway, without money, he worked menial jobs and attended a university for two years. His sweetheart had left Vietnam before Saigon's fall. He learned she was in the United States and wrote asking her to join him in Norway. She did. They were married there. The new bride returned to the States and her husband came later as a legal immigrant to our country.

He arrived with dreams and hope for a better life and started a mom-and-pop store. When he sold it for a profit, he bought two liquor stores. Meanwhile, he entered law school and obtained a law degree in 1989. He also had attained a real estate broker's license. Life was good. When California's real estate values took a dive in 1990, he went broke.

A drop in the economy doesn't stop a guy who survived a North Vietnamese reeducation camp. My new fishing buddy is now back on top. He lives here with his wife and their youngest son.

He loves to fish and accepts the days he doesn't catch anything as part of life. I watch him as he stands aloof, deep in thought, with his coffee, a relaxed face and patience. He appreciates the tranquility that surrounds us. His journey to San Clemente was far more dangerous than mine. I'm glad he took it. More important, I'm glad he made it.

That's the view from the pier.

WEDDING ANNIVERSARY

From its beginning to its end marriage creates a unique relationship. I was reminded of this over the last couple of weeks as I attended a neighbor's fiftieth wedding celebration and our daughter's bridal shower. One reflected appreciation, the other anticipation.

A few weeks ago, my neighbor and pier pal, affectionately known as "Blind Jim," and his wife, celebrated their fifty-year marriage. I went to their party twice. See, Cora handles our social calendar, such as it is. On October 19th, she reminded me to come home early because the fifty-year celebration started at seven. I arrived as ordered, put on my best suit and asked for instructions.

"To the Marriott at Dana Point," Cora directed.

We zipped over and arrived at five minutes to seven. I parked the car and we entered the lobby in anticipation of a great event. As I carried our gift past the doorman, he asked, "Going to the birthday party?"

"No, the fiftieth wedding anniversary," I answered. He looked puzzled.

When we inquired at the hotel counter for the location of the gathering, the clerk couldn't find a listing. "Are you sure?" Cora asked.

He nodded with certainty. I told Cora to stay put and dashed back to the car to check the invitation. Aha! I solved the mystery. The party was at the DoubleTree in Capistrano Beach. I returned for Cora. As we entered our vehicle, she said apologetically, "I don't know why I thought it was at the Marriott." I shrugged my shoulders not understanding how anyone could make such a mistake.

We sped to the DoubleTree and the valet parked our car. Only a few minutes late I figured as we entered the hotel. We asked the clerk for the location of the fiftieth wedding

party. She looked at us with a blank stare. "We don't have anything tonight," she said.

"You must," Cora pleaded. The clerk checked with the manager.

She returned with a knowing look, "No, nothing tonight," she said apologetically.

How could this be happening, I thought as I went back to the car to get the invitation and prove them wrong. Our car had already been parked, so I searched the parking structure to find it. At the car, I carefully checked the invitation for the date. I had failed to do that at the Marriott. Holy mole! The party was next week. How did I miss that?

Well, we finally got it right the next Friday and took the ribbing from guests who by this time had heard of our dry run the week before. The real party was great. The celebrants' children treated us to photo slides of their parents who married during World War II. Their love for each other and family was reflected in every slide. We all felt the devotion that evening as the children and grandchildren lauded their parents and grandparents. The pier pals echoed the same feelings. Yes, everyone recognized what fifty years of hard work, dedication and love can yield.

Two weeks later, I watched our youngest daughter, Andrea, at her bridal shower. Family and gifts surrounded the young couple as she and her fiancé, Chris, sat beaming. I thought of my pier pal and his wife. They had married during a war and did a lot better than just survive. I prayed Andrea and Chris would do the same. Their love will be tested over the years, just as my pier pal and his lovely wife had been.

If Chris and Andrea work at it, they will create a beautiful new entity, one they won't see but only feel. It is built out of respect for each other, patience, and a sense of humor and bound together by love. Its rewards come with moments that blend their talents taking them to new heights.

Eventually, the two will think as one or know why they don't and respect the difference. They may even arrive at a party one week ahead of time because of a partner's mistake and not be upset. That's when they will know that the creature they created takes over and makes them laugh about it.

That's the view from the pier.

BIRTHDAYS

By the time you become a grandfather, the only birthdays you get invited to are the ones for persons over sixty or under six. Even then, gender can prevent an invitation.

Recently, my granddaughter Marisa announced no boys would be allowed at her four-year-old birthday party. I asked if I could come. She answered, "You're a boy, Papa."

"What about your father? He's a boy."

"He's doing the piñata," she answered, justifying his attendance.

"What if I dress like a girl?"

"You're a boy Papa, no boys allowed."

Well, what the heck, Marisa was entitled to have her party the way she wanted it. Besides, Cora would report back on the all-girls party.

Cora and I recently went to two surprise birthday parties for two longtime friends. That's why I wasn't fishing last Saturday. The two honorees were surprised and cried. You tend to do that if you're sixty or over. Friends and relatives shared stories. Tears and laughter were abundant.

As I sat there enjoying the festivities, I was struck with the notion of how much emphasis we place on birthdays. It's funny. We celebrate a day none of us actually remember. Our parents tell us about it. But as I listened to the stories, I began to understand birthdays' importance. They are days to review personal history. The more birthdays, the more history.

That's why I enjoyed talking to a favorite pier pal who turned ninety-six a couple of weeks ago and passed away twelve hours later. He was the friendliest and most likeable

gentleman that walked the pier. We met fourteen years ago when I started fishing there. He walked the pier every day until recent times when two broken hips stopped him.

Before then, he'd stop and chat. We would talk about the events of the day, politics and fishing. He claimed he bought a new pole and was going to join me one day.

Born in Sweden, he had a slight accent. His memory was sharp as a hook as he pulled up tales from his youth and life. He was a walking history book. What I remember most was how young his mind stayed. I once commented, "You're looking great."

"Feel twenty years younger!" he said.

That was his secret: feeling younger. He appreciated every day and taught me the lesson. Each day reminded him of a prior one he had lived. I was fascinated.

Eventually he went on dialysis. The normal life span is a few years, but he hung in for over seven. But that was him. In his later years he understood life. That's what a stack of birthdays does. They allow us to view life against a background of experiences and he had many.

Medical technology has allowed more persons in this country to reach the century mark. As a society, we haven't quite figured out what to do with them. Children never thought parents would live so long and senior centers never contemplated seniors this old.

There's a growing wealth of experiences living amongst us that we shouldn't ignore. We now have history treasures untapped to pass on to future generations. My pier pal placed life in perspective for me. He had seen wars, depressions, and good times; experienced joy and sorrow; and knew the value of each. I began to understand why I like the pier and why he came out everyday . . . tranquility.

He was cremated and his ashes scattered at sea. I suspect he'll hang out at the pier like he used to. Who knows, he might talk to me again in case I forget his lessons.

Marisa occasionally joins me to catch a fish. Next time she does, I'm going to tell her about my pier pal and all the birthdays he had. Maybe she'll invite me to hers next time.

That's the view from the pier.

WOODIES

One of the features of the annual Ocean Festival at San Clemente is the arrival of the "woodies" that are driven onto the pier in the morning and remain displayed for six hours each day of the weekend festival. As a longtime angler, I resented the wood-paneled cars and their owners. They deprived us of prime fishing locations at the pier rails.

This becomes particularly upsetting during the fishing tournament that takes place on Sunday from 6:30 a.m. until noon. Hey, it's tough trying to catch fish, but when folks attracted by the woodies crowd the pier rail to see our catch, they put pressure on us. I fish to relax, not to put pressure on myself. Nobody wants to be the guy that everyone points to, saying, "That's the guy that lost the big fish." Consequently, many regulars stay home during the festival. I feel obligated to support it and so enter the fishing tournament. No, I didn't win a prize this year. In fact, I didn't catch a fish big enough to even submit for consideration. But the lack of action did give me time to think. I looked around me and saw the activities on the beach and pier—anglers, swimmers, surfers and runners doing their thing free from formal land attire. Laughter, music and gleeful conversations filled the air as strollers sauntered by.

I remembered the big oil spill in the Gulf of Mexico and speculated on the impact and disaster such a thing would have on our lives here. I began to have a stronger appreciation for a clean ocean and all the joys that comes with it. A line in a song came to mind, "You don't know what you have until it becomes a have-not."

Then I focused on the woodies parked along the pier railings and my dislike for them and their owners faded. I saw how clean and shiny each vehicle appeared, and its owner beamed with pride. Folks I initially viewed as show-offs with big toys I began to see as committed historians preserving our country's past on wheels so that we would not forget those days of the past.

Wooden carriages go back to Holland around 1600, when chariots on land carried up to 28 people. The concept may go back further than that in China. By 1789 a U.S. patent for a self-propelled carriage was recorded. Eventually, Oliver Evans was commissioned by Philadelphia to build an authentic amphibious vehicle. By 1924, Renault had introduced a wood-sided vehicle. The 1930s brought on more wood-sided autos. The price for a coupe was $399 and a wagon cost $565. Woodies in those days were owned by comics like Laurel and Hardy and other movie stars. Wooden station wagons became favorites for baby boomers and growing families. Eventually, metal replaced wood sides because metal took less maintenance. During the forties and fifties woodies became identified with beaches and surfers. Today, those models stand as reminders of days when we were a more naive nation. Woodies are a visual icon of an era.

I returned home at the end of the day without a fish, but with an appreciation for a clean sea and the preservation of the past. I no longer dislike woody owners. They have patience, some money and a commitment to restore our past inventions so we at the present may enjoy them. In a way they are like fishermen. Patience is a required ingredient. The search for a missing auto part can be as frustrating as trying to catch a fish. But when the part is found or a fish is caught, all the time spent was worth it.

That's the view from the pier.

THREE AMIGOS

Three lives were wrapped up in one week and put away. The first was Steve Kemiji. We met in Sacramento. I was to be the DMV's director in Jerry Brown's first administration as governor. Steve also arrived and became instrumental in providing qualified interpreters for hearings under the new Farm Labor Law. We both lived in Davis and became friends because of our mutual interests in family, politics and the Latino community. Maria, his wife, passed away many years ago and we moved back to Southern California. Steve remained up north, but we stayed in touch by phone and later through the Internet. We discussed family, life and politics over the years. Each conversation was as if we had just spoken the day before. Finally, his weak lungs couldn't function. His loving children were by his bedside when he checked out.

The second life that departed was that of Fred Velasco. He and Cora were classmates in high school. His father was a tailor in downtown L.A. and Fred joined him. He became my tailor when I became a lawyer in 1960. His extended credit to a young attorney with a family starting a solo practice was God sent. Fred taught me how to buy suits and how to take care of them. He later would become the unofficial tailor of the L.A. Lakers, outfitting coach Pat Riley and many of the players. When I ran for a political office, he came to my aid. I didn't win, but I was the best-dressed candidate. I enjoyed buying suits from Fred. We discussed politics and life in general. When he retired, I hated buying suits. Fred had spoiled me. Five years ago Fred had a lung transplant. He took up to sixty pills a day to convince his body to accept the new lung. But after five years battling his body's resistance, Fred left tired but at peace.

The third life that left was that of Armando Campero. I always called him by his last name. He was a student of Diego Rivera. Campero came to Los Angeles in the sixties to seek his fortune painting murals. When we met and he told me of his dream, I laughed and said, "They don't paint murals here in the United States. They use walls for advertising."

But he stayed anyway, painted and tried selling his paintings. His enthusiasm encouraged me to return to painting. When I and some fellow attorneys bought a small Los Angeles law building, we commissioned him to do a mural in our narrow lobby. I told him we didn't have much money. Campero didn't care. "You have given me a wall!" he said embracing me as if we had given him the ceiling of the Sistine Chapel. At the unveiling of our mural, county officials were impressed. They commissioned him to adorn many walls in county buildings. He lived and breathed art. Nothing else mattered. Cancer finally cleared his palette, but his art survives.

So in one week, three of my friends have gone. Death comes not as a surprise. By the time you reach my age, you have seen it many times. It is never pleasant. The loss always brings sorrow. But eventually that leaves. What remains are the memories and the echoes of voices and laughter. Although Steve, Fred and Campero never joined me out on the pier to fish, they will accompany me now with my fishing poles. If you see me smiling looking out at the sea, or maybe talking to no one visible, don't be alarmed. I'll be remembering a conversation with Steve, or getting fitted for a suit by Fred, or asking Campero what should I do to enhance one of my paintings.

That's the view from the pier.

A GOOD MORNING

The morning is overcast as I stroll out to the pier Sunday at 7:00 a.m. carrying two poles and fishing gear. I stop at the café across the street from the pier and get a decaf coffee. The waitress welcomes me and wants all the fish I catch. I'll be lucky to get a bite.

I wave to Paul Gavin, the artist, who is setting up his paintings in front of the Fisherman's Restaurant at the start of the pier. He is there every weekend with his paintings that capture the essence of San Clemente.

My ears are filled with the sound of the pounding waves as they break about fifty yards from the shoreline and white foam covers the last forty yards into the shore. I check the water on the north side as white water with beautiful moving designs disappears into the sand surrounding the pillars holding up the Fisherman's. Yesterday, the white water had too much seaweed to fish there.

I go further out past the lifeguard tower and meet another local angler, but he's not fishing today. Not a good sign for me, because he studies the tide and weather reports and picks the days he will fish after analyzing all that information. I like to see him fishing because it boosts my confidence.

I set up on the north side of the pier just before the waves start to break. I'm past the surfers. The swells are huge. Should be some fish here I figure. The first pole I use is the one my dad left me, and I cast the line out about twenty yards with live ghost shrimp on the hook. This shrimp is supposed be like candy for fish. Experience tells me that a lot of fish are on sugar free diets. I bait my second pole with a lugworm and cast the line closer to the pier. The swells pull my lines and my poles bend. I know enough to know the sea did it, not fish.

Marie Burke, a regular pier pal, and Pierre and Joan, two annual snowbirds from the east, wander out. Pierre and Joan will be going home this week and won't return next year. Years are catching up to them they say. I will miss them. We all talk and my dad's pole looks like a fish is on. I reel in a thirteen-inch spot fin croaker, good enough for a fish taco. Pierre and Joan are thrilled that they saw me actually catch a fish. Tom and Sue Bell, two other pier regulars, arrive and check out my catch. I tell them that I need to land Cora a fish, because she gets upset when I eat a fish taco alone. Phil, my son arrives from his morning run on the beach trail. When the pier pals depart Phil remains.

He watches as I keep reeling in my lines, taking off the kelp and tossing out the line again and again. Phil's not a fisherman and I begin to wonder why I am. I am losing bait to the kelp and I keep tossing my line out for Cora's fish. Phil and I share our work adventures over the past week. I enjoy keeping abreast of his career as a songwriter, record producer and worship leader. I continue to ask why he won't use my voice on one of his recordings? He tells me not to get discouraged. We laugh. Time to head home for breakfast with Cora.

As we trudge up to our cars in the parking lot, I think of my two-hour stay on the pier. Fresh air, pounding waves, pier pals, one fish and a son willing to put up with an old man trying to catch fish. It doesn't get any better than that.

That's the view from the pier.

PIERS

"All piers are not created equal," a friend of mine told me. She may be right, but they're similar. Recently, my wife Cora and I drove up the central coast of California to see Hearst Castle. About a quarter of a mile from the entrance road, there's a pier. It's small, about a hundred-plus feet long, built to receive treasures for the castle brought over the sea by ships.

Seeing the pier, I had to walk it. I can't stroll by the mouth of a pier and not journey out. That's like seeing salsa and chips and not tasting them. It ain't going to happen.

I recognized the smell—the sea, seaweed, damp wood and fish. The sounds were the same, seagulls calling from above and little waves slapping the pilings below. The fishermen leaned against the old wooden rail, keeping eyes on poles and hoping. The clothes held true to anglers' fashions—grubby, old and faded.

"How's it going? Any luck?" I asked.

"Yep, fish have it."

I moved on to the end where another hopeful stood. We talked for a few minutes and I asked what's usually caught in the water there. "You mean what they say or what's factual?" I smiled and nodded my head.

Later, coming home down the coast, we decided to stop at other piers and check them out. At Morro Bay, I saw an old salt at the end of the pier by himself. I felt I knew him as if I had seen him a hundred times fishing somewhere. He had two lines in the water and a cart with everything he'd need to haul up a fish foolish enough to take the bait.

"How's it going?" I asked.

He didn't answer as he looked at me expressionless from behind dark glasses. I understood. He wasn't there to play twenty questions with tourists. I nodded and wished him well.

As I walked back to our car, I got to thinking about piers. They're like a toe in the ocean testing the water. I didn't see any caught fish on the boardwalks during my visit, but on a pier that doesn't matter. There are more important things happening. It's a coastal campus for learning about life. At each pier I saw fathers with children, teaching them how to fish and more.

I see that here on the weekends at the San Clemente Pier. Fathers come with poles and excited children, their students. I enjoy overhearing the conversations as class star ts.

"Dad, have I caught a fish yet?"

"No, be patient."

"How will I know?"

"You'll feel a tug on your line."

"Okay . . . Dad, I feel a tug on my line."

The pole doesn't move. "Son, there's no fish. Leave the line in the water, be patient."

"How do I know the bait's still there?"

"It is, don't worry."

"Have I had a tug yet, Dad?"

Dialogue continues with fathers answering questions, trying to fish. Nothing on a pier is ruled by a clock. Time becomes an observer not the leader. There aren't many places left for this to happen. Places of the past are gone or have become expensive. Disneyland and the like are time-driven from their rides to their food.

I have to admit, pier fishing doesn't provide overwhelming action. There is more waiting than doing. But maybe that's what the Big Fisherman had in mind for us mortals.

If fish were tugging at our line all the time, we wouldn't pay attention to the beautiful scene around us and contemplate life. Nor would there be the time for fathers and children to talk. Smart fathers know that.

They answer questions and after awhile questions stop. In the silence something is happening—the creation of a memory. Father and child stand and enjoy its silent growth. Fish around piers are under strict orders by Mother Nature during this quality time, "Leave the bait alone." Eventually the ban gets lifted, allowing fish to bite.

When father and child depart, with poles in hand and maybe a fish, I hear, "Dad can we come back?"

"Sure . . . one of these days."

I don't know if they will, it doesn't really matter. For the rest of that father's life, he'll hear, "Dad, remember when we went fishing on the pier?" You bet he does.

That's the view from the pier.

131 Avenida Navarro, San Clemente, CA 91672
949-940-8113

PART TWO: THE SEARCH

Living is an exploration of this world, its wonders and all who occupy it. Here are some of my conclusions.

The First Heartbreak—*In our search of life we encounter setbacks. One such setback is a broken heart. This painting attempts to depict that first heartbreak and the comfort provided by a father.*

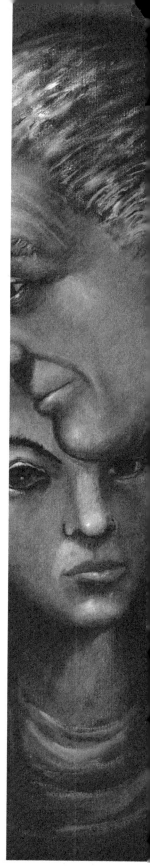

LOST POUNDS

Most men pick up weight after they get married. I was no exception. The pounds came without me paying much attention. Sure, I had to get larger-sized suits but I accused my tailor of selling me ones that shrunk. I accepted the increased poundage as part of getting older and being happy.

Every year after Thanksgiving and too many Christmas tamales, I thought of losing weight. January TV commercials advertising diets and exercise machines reminded me of my increasing bulk. Yet I did nothing more than make New Year's resolutions and break them by February.

In fact, I convinced myself that I was actually helping people by taking on a few pounds. I created a theory on the pier while waiting for my fishing pole to bend. See, the earth's weight must remain constant to stay in the right orbit around the sun. Any loss of substantial weight can throw our planet off its course. A collision with another heavenly body would be disastrous.

So when people would say to me, "I lost five pounds," or "I lost fifteen," I wondered where did those pounds go? I mean if everybody was losing them, wouldn't the earth lose its weight? What would happen if all the people in the world just lost one pound at the same time? We're talking about tons and tons! Disaster. Yet, nothing ever happened. Why not?

I found the solution when I stepped on a scale a couple of years back. The day before, I had been talking to a friend who had dropped ten pounds. When I weighed myself the next day, I had gained four. I couldn't figure how that could have happened. Then it dawned on me. I got them from my bragging buddy. The pounds had to go somewhere. He was the grantor and I was the unknowing grantee. I accepted my newfound role as contributing to the safety of humanity. Every pound I gained was helping folks who were

32

selfishly shedding theirs.

Well, I just turned seventy. I'm a youngster to some folks that walk the pier every morning. One of my favorite pier pals is ninety-one. As I've become more observant of senior men, I've noticed one thing. You don't see many old fat guys. The only one I know of is Santa Claus, and he only makes it out of his house once a year at night when no one can see him.

Cora has me on a diet now. I'm losing weight. I walk up the hill from the pier without stopping to catch my breath. Yep, I feel better. No more fried tacos, tortillas, chips and bread. Even my grandchildren's favorite, fish tacos from the fish I catch out on the pier, will lose its dominance on my plate. Vegetables rule.

At lunch in Los Angeles restaurants, I've noticed that my clients don't eat bread either. A restaurant owner told me that his bread supplier was complaining. Orders were down. A food revolution is under way. Still, old habits are hard to break. The test for me was the Super Bowl. Chips and nachos everywhere but I behaved. Salsa doesn't taste as good on celery sticks but I can live with it. After all, that's the goal, living.

Since God gives an extra day of life for each day a person fishes, Cora figures I better enjoy the extra time with less weight. My grandchildren will still have their beloved fish tacos when they come over. I'll get the same kick watching them devour my catch and listening to them brag about how many they ate. After all, they're picking up the pounds that I lost. Someone has to do it.

That's the view from the pier.

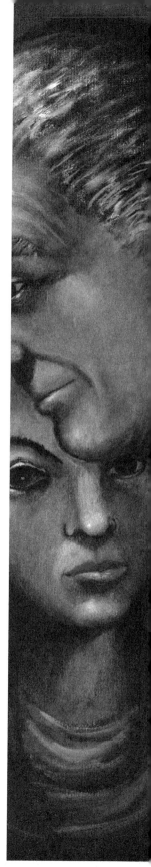

TRUE LOVE

Last week, Cora and I lunched with Licha Eggli on the pier. We first met her in the sixties. Now at the Fisherman's Restaurant, the sunlight danced on top of a calm sea. I could see Licha enjoyed the scene. "What brought you to the U.S.?" I asked.

"Amor," she sighed and spoke in Spanish of her small village, La Aventosa, Mexico. It had no roads, electricity nor plumbing. When she was fourteen, a Swiss stranger came for vacation. After a week, he needed his clothes washed. She agreed to wash them in the river. He held her hand when he placed some pesos in it for payment.

The next summer, the Swiss returned and asked if she remembered him. She didn't. This time, besides paying Licha for washed clothes, he taught her to drive his car. Then he left.

He returned the next year and asked Licha's father for permission to court her. The father turned him down. The Swiss was twenty years older than Licha.

Undaunted, the Swiss returned the following year. "I was so young and had no special feelings toward him," Licha recalled. He brought gifts for everyone. In the meantime, she attended school at Salina Cruz, a nearby town. She learned to read and write.

When the Swiss reappeared again, he told Licha that at eighteen she could legally make up her own mind. If she decided not to go with him, he would never return. His love and persistence were rewarded. Her family acquiesced and Jacob took his new bride to the bustling city of San Francisco. The tall buildings, crowds and pace frightened his her.

Jacob worked for an international mining company and was called back to Switzerland. He told Licha they would go by boat. "The only boats I knew were our village boats," Licha explained. "Then, I saw the Queen Mary! He bought me clothes for the trip and we ate at tables with many forks and spoons. I couldn't believe what was happening. But he taught me what to wear and which forks and spoons to use."

Once in Switzerland, Licha, a product of tropical climate, found she couldn't stand the cold. Jacob saw she was miserable. They returned to California and eventually to L.A. where a cousin from La Aventosa lived. She had married an Americano.

By now, Licha had learned English and how to use a checkbook. Fifteen years after their wedding, Jacob had cancer. Licha's eyes watered as she continued with her story.

Jacob returned to Switzerland to spend his last months. She and their children would join him when school finished. Death didn't wait. His family offered to care for her and the children but Licha returned to L.A.

She overcame the new challenge. Her children are now grown and married. The oldest, Liz, lives in Dana Point.

Licha, now a grandmother, occasionally visits La Aventosa. When there, she wanders out to a small river where she washed clothes for a Swiss stranger. He never let a different culture, language, age or distance deter him from pursuing his love, nor did she ever abandon their dream.

That's the view from the pier.

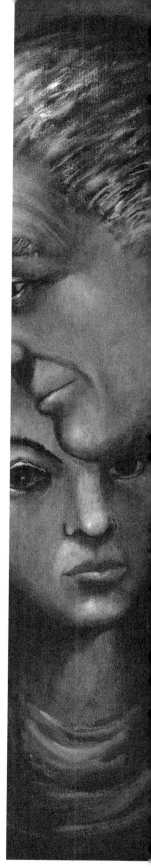

PLEIN AIR

My two worlds, law and art, collided when the San Clemente Art Association (SCAA) had its annual plein air art contest two weeks ago. The event invites artists to compete for ten thousand dollars in prizes. Contestants pay a fee and have a week to submit two paintings of San Clemente no larger than 22" x 24" when framed. The work must be done outdoors (plein air). I innocently entered.

I commenced painting on Sunday at the pier and set up next to the Fisherman's Restaurant. This was my first plein air venture. I felt like Van Gogh with both ears. If I painted for three hours every morning before going to L.A. I figured I'd meet the deadline.

Monday afternoon, a client needed a federal injunction. Duty called and I worked two days and a night. Fortunately, the crisis passed, so on Thursday, I returned to my art world and painted twelve hours straight on the pier!

Tourists stopped and talked as I worked to meet the deadline. Pier pals offered me five bucks for the painting if I threw in the easel. Later, another one offered me twenty-five dollars if he could make payments. My legs ached. Painting was hard work.

I had also entered the Quick Draw Contest scheduled for Friday. Contestants assembled at the Ole Hanson Beach Club. Artists were sprinkled all over the place waiting for the starting 10:00 a.m. horn.

The same canvas size restrictions applied, but everyone came with really small canvases. I lugged in a 16" x 20" piece. How did I expect to paint a decent picture on a 16" x 20" canvas in two hours? What was I thinking?

I set up near the train tracks far enough away so trains wouldn't hit me when they came whistling by. The starting horn sounded and the Quick Draw competition was on.

I threw paint on canvas like a possessed house painter. "Come on Sillas, you have only two hours," I said. My sky was done and I worked on the foliage. Down the tracks a northbound train headed toward me. I could see that it kicked up dust. Not to worry. I turned my back on the train as it passed by.

Then with brush and palette in hand, I turned to face my canvas. It was gone! My easel stood buck-naked. Someone in the train must have stolen my masterpiece. I looked to my right and left but no painting. I took steps back while looking ahead on the ground for my canvas. On the next step back, I found my painting. I had stepped on it. My footprint was imbedded in my finished sky. I quickly picked up the canvas and dusted off the gravel. Oh man, the clock was ticking and here I was with gravel and a footprint in the sky. Then I thought of the song "Ghost Riders in the Sky" and laughed. I had unintentionally made my work into a mixed medium abstract.

Now, I was really behind. Only thirty minutes left and one half of the canvas hadn't been touched yet. Just then my cell phone rang. No. Justice can't be calling now.

"Hello?" I answered quickly while getting paint on my phone.

"How's it going?" It was Cora's sweet voice.

"I can't talk to you now," I growled, trying to wipe the paint off the phone and get back to my challenge.

"Okay," she answered apologetically, making me feel like a heel. Now I know why Van Gogh cut off his ear.

I returned to painting with an abandonment of any artistic eye. To cover the canvas was my sole goal. I made it and turned in my effort as the ending horn sounded. Nah, I didn't win a prize, but I would have if they had one for being the dumbest plein air artist.

That's the view from the pier.

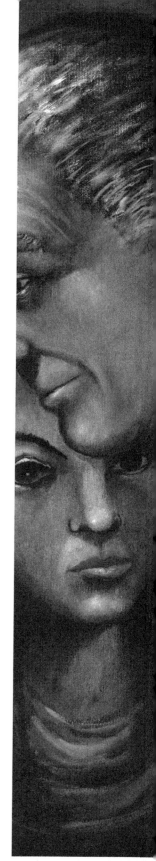

TOMBSTONES

Cora and I are at that stage in life where we recognize we have fewer years remaining than those we've lived. Consequently, we don't throw away cemetery advertisements anymore. We save them. In the meantime, we have engaged in discussions regarding our inevitable departure from earth. Planning your own funeral is about as pleasant as writing your will except you are not distributing assets, only ashes or a body.

Longtime married couples deal with their bodies as if they were one. That's Cora and me. We're trying to figure out whether to be buried or cremated. We haven't made a decision yet. Nor have we made any decision as to where in San Clemente we want our remains to rest. Since Debbie, our oldest daughter, married into the Nell family, which received a land grant from William Penn in the 1600s, she is assured of a free plot in the Nells' family cemetery. Our loving son-in-law, Craig, has told Cora and me that we have a standing invitation to be buried there without charge. Cora nixed the Pennsylvania burial. I thought it was great, because future visitors would wonder how a Spanish surname like Sillas landed in a William Penn land grant cemetery?

I have a thing about tombstones. This has come out in my discussions with Cora. During our dialog we assumed that we'd be buried together. Then the lawyer in me took over. I pointed out that if we didn't die together, one of us would be a surviving spouse. I've seen too many tombstones with an engraved husband's name, date of birth and death, and then a space for the wife's name to be engraved when she passes away. The assumption of both spouses was that at the survivor's death she would be buried with her deceased husband. Too many unfinished tombstones reveal that some fellows have been waiting a long time for their respective wives. Where are they? Maybe some are still alive because their deceased husbands were much older than they. That's possible but not probable. Maybe the wives lived to be more than a hundred years of age? That's possible but not probable. The likelihood is that the wives are buried somewhere else. Maybe some really didn't like their husbands, didn't want to spend any more time with them dead or alive, but didn't want to have an argument with the guy on his deathbed.

I suspect however, that many remarried and are lying with a new dead husband or may be alone waiting for their second husband to join them. In either event, there is a bunch of fellows in cemeteries with unfinished tombstones.

I don't have a problem with Cora remarrying after I'm gone. She should do whatever she wants to make her happy. I just don't want people that I don't know laughing at my gravesite because I appear to be waiting for Cora and she ain't coming. I had enough people laugh at me when I was alive. I don't need them laughing at me when I'm dead.

So I came up with the revocable tombstone policy. Whoever goes first will have a tombstone with space for the living spouse, but if the survivor changes his or her mind about joining the deceased spouse that's okay. All the survivor needs to do is notify the cemetery where the deceased spouse lies. The cemetery would then be obligated to remove the unfinished tombstone and replace it with the sole name of the deceased lying in the ground. Then future observers would believe the deceased is peacefully resting and not waiting for anyone. I presented my idea to Cora. She looked at me as if I was nuts and said, "Whatever makes you happy while you're alive, dear."

That's the view from the pier.

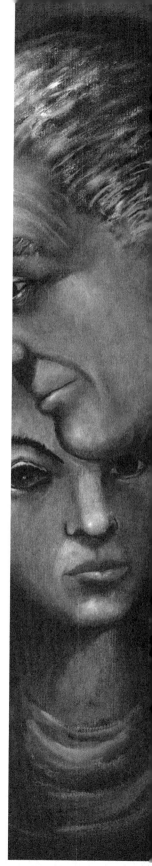

HUGS

I met with two folks from UCLA the other day. One of them I have known for over a decade. We hugged upon his arrival. The other gentleman I was meeting for the first time. We shook hands. After an hour-long meeting, they departed. On this occasion, I hugged them both. That's when I began to think about hugs. I'm a hugger and have been all my life. Those I hug are "huggees." I keep my eyes out for hugs, who gives them and who gets them.

Riding the train weekly, I see plenty of folks saying hello and goodbye. Some greetings and departures come with hugs and some don't. I wonder why the difference? Is it the relationship of the individuals, the individuals themselves, their culture or the times we live in?

I decided to take an inventory of the number of folks I hug. Well, Cora tops the list, but admittedly I don't hug her enough. Grandchildren get hugs whether they want them or not. I invite them as I hold out my arms to embrace them. They range from thirty-five years of age to six years old. Depending on their ages, they react differently, but by the time they reach twelve, they know that I'm going to hug them. They accept the inevitable. This result comes only after my children have reminded their offspring to hug and kiss grandpa at every family gathering. The function starts as a duty, evolves into habit and hopefully ends as an act of affection.

My children and their spouses get hugs whether male or female. I always kiss the females. On a few occasions, I have kissed son and sons-in-law. I do admit that kissing a man's unshaved cheek is different from a woman's smooth face. My siblings and their spouses get hugs. Next come aunts, uncles, cousins, nieces and nephews, they all get hugs. In-laws get them if they want them. Comadres and compadres (godparents to my children or I'm a godparent to their children) get squeezes too. The truth of the matter is if you are familia you get a hug. Hugs come at every meeting and farewell. That's why Mexican goodbyes take so long.

Checking my inventory of huggees, I realized a few friends are included. Yet, some longtime friends don't get hugs. It's because they don't feel comfortable getting one. Some folks accept hugging; others don't. I respect that. At the work place, one has to be careful. Go around hugging folks and you've got a sexual harassment claim against you.

My dad was of the old macho school and taught me its rules—men don't cry, etc. In his later years, he hugged and kissed me at every meeting. I understood. It was then I decided I'd start my hugging earlier in life.

There is nothing like putting your arms around a loved one and, by the gesture alone, conveying that he or she is something special. Symbolically, it conveys trust and that there are no barriers between the hugger and huggee. If so, at that moment they have been put aside. When was the last time you hugged someone?

Admittedly, when meeting someone for the first time it's difficult to determine if a person likes an embrace or not. Check the eyes. Are they smiling? Spread your arms out. If the subject doesn't move toward you, pretend you are stretching.

I think if we did more hugging in this world there would be less conflict. It's tough to hit someone when they have their arms around you. As a hugger in a non-hugging world, I walk around like a chile addict sucking on an empty salsa bottle. Need a hug? Let me know. I'm always looking for a new huggee.

That's the view from the pier.

KELLER WILLIAMS
OC COASTAL REALTY

Steve Carrico

Keller Williams
OC Coastal
111 Via Pico Plaza
San Clemente
92672

949-636-5321

EMAIL:
Sold@SteveCarrico.com
WEBSITE:
www.SteveCarrico.com

*Congratulations on your book Herman.
I've been encouraged, humbled, humored, and
inspired by our many days on the pier hearing
"your view"*

Steve Carrico

**As a Top Producing Associate of the highest
ranked Real Estate brokerage in San Clemente,
my objective is to serve the residents of the
community at the highest level.**

**Licensed since 1998
Specializing in Single Family Ocean
View Homes**

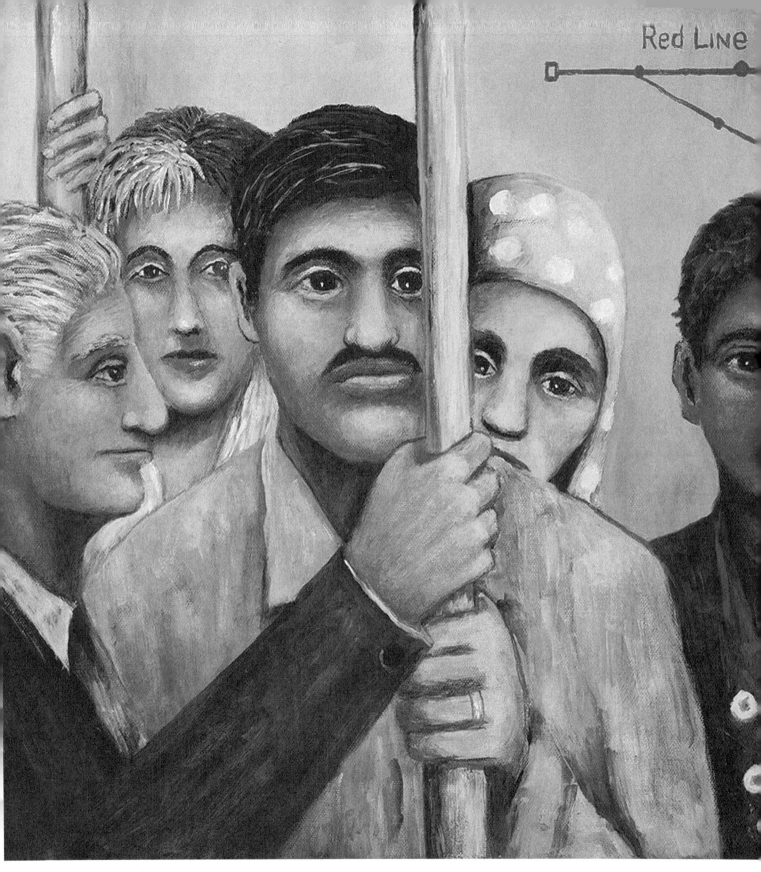

Red Line

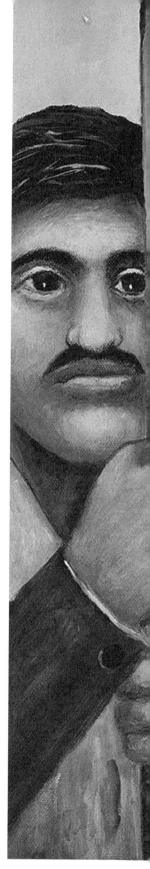

PART THREE: POLITICS

When I entered college, I learned for the first time that there was something called political science. Since I had been high school student body president, I decided to make political science my major. After graduating with a B.A. in political science and finding no country willing to let me lead it, I went to law school. But my love of politics never left me. After running twice as a losing statewide candidate in the seventies, serving as the Secretary of the California Democratic Party, getting appointed by Governor Jerry Brown as the Director of the Department of Motor Vehicles, and being appointed a United States Attorney by President Jimmy Carter, I feel as competent as anyone else to comment on what we call politics.

Hanging On—*I ride the subway to my Los Angeles law office with a diverse group. The thought occurs to me that we are all in this world together, hanging on, in spite of politics.*

45

OLD SOLDIERS

Seeing the D-Day celebration and watching former political enemies embrace each other at President Ronald Reagan's memorial got me to thinking. Time heals wounds like sandy beaches absorb angry waves. But what about the young lives that were lost during the period of hostility?

At the end of World War II, we sighed believing it was the war that ended all wars. Yet, since then, the U.S. has been involved in three major wars not to mention several skirmishes. I have reluctantly come to the conclusion that conflicts will always be with us. Nations' leaders aren't interested in anger management.

If war is inevitable, let's examine who are the soldiers. Today, countries send young adults believed to be the physically best to fight. Too many return in long boxes.

Their deaths leave a vacuum and mourning families behind. Youngsters grow up knowing only one parent and learning the missing one was a hero. The truth of the matter is that we're sending the wrong age group to fight!

Send the old folks to war. Yeah, I know that means me, but think about what could happen if we seniors were on the front lines. First, we aren't about to rush into things. You know what I mean? If some general orders us to take a hill, we'd ask questions first. "Do we really need it?" Some of us might have an alternative, such as, "How about going around it?"

If we're convinced that possession of the real estate is really necessary, that's when our experience kicks in. We'd march out under a flag of truce to talk to the enemy first. Time to talk turkey. See if we can cut a deal. What's their price? Will they take payments? Think of all the installment contracts we seniors have had in our lifetime. You think we aren't savvy about getting the best terms?

If the enemy doesn't want to sell the real estate outright, how about a lease? The term would just be until the end of the war anyway. If the enemy isn't interested in a lease, then maybe we could compete for the site. Poker, dominoes, chess, checkers, bingo or Monopoly produce winners without the bloodshed. If the real estate in question is really important we could have a tournament. We seniors enjoy those. Sure, we'd have uniforms. The media needs to know who is winning.

If all of this fails, then and only then would we engage in a shooting war. It would be possible that by that time the real estate is no longer that important. If still critical for victory, then we'd do what we've got to do. With today's technology, we'd press the right buttons and clear the hill for our occupation. Sure, some of us might not make it back. Heck, we've done it all anyway—played, worked, married, had children and grandchildren. What did we miss? Besides, what grandparent wouldn't lay down his or her life for children and grandchildren? In many cases, calling on the aged to fight wars solves a problem for many seniors: "What's for dinner?" That becomes the military's problem. Also, some seniors feel unwanted and unappreciated in this youth-focused society. Knowing that the military still wants us restores a feeling of worth. Besides, wars will cost less. Seniors don't eat that much meat and we are on Social Security. When Friday nights roll around, sergeants won't worry about the troops. We're in bed by ten. Here's the beauty of my idea. After the war, each country would still have its brightest and most productive population for the future. Besides, an aged army might bring on a forced peace. What world leader would send grandparents to fight a war? His or her parents would ask, "Are you crazy?" Somebody needs to ask that question.

That's the view from the pier.

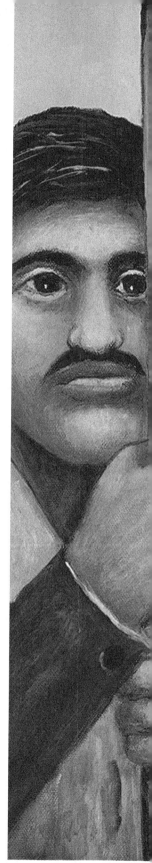

DA MAYOR

I was in the car driving when I first heard the news that the former mayor of Los Angeles, Tom Bradley, was dead. For the rest of the trip, my mind traveled back to the 1960s when I first met him. The 1965 Watts Riots were on everybody's mind then and there was a concern among Los Angeles officials that East Los Angeles, with its heavy Latino population, would blow up next. The establishment set up meetings with the Latino community and city councilman Tom Bradley attended one. I was a young lawyer and impressed with his demeanor and calmness.

When he ran for mayor in 1969, I volunteered to help head up the Latino effort. We were all new to politics and it was a tough haul. No one believed that an African American could be elected Mayor of Los Angeles. They were right then, we lost.

Tom Bradley tried again in 1973. I joined him as before. Same opponent, different results. On election night we gathered at a large hall on Washington Boulevard in Los Angeles. As election results came in, it was clear that it would be a close race. About 11:30 p.m., Tom Bradley went ahead in the count and the place went wild. The band played louder, cheers were deafening, and people were hugging each other and dancing. Tears of joy flowed down the different shades of faces gathered that night, including mine.

I've been to many campaigns' headquarters on election nights since, losers and winners. None compared with the raw emotion that saturated the air that historical evening in 1973. The celebration was about more than that election. This was a major breakthrough for all of California. Old folks were crying, knowing their grandchildren's dreams could become reality as theirs did. Another racial barrier flushed away.

Later, after his inauguration, there followed an elaborate reception at the Dorothy Chandler Pavilion for supporters. The event was Los Angeles showing off with finger food, champagne and chamber music. Politicians, lobbyists and power people roamed looking for the next deal or compromise.

Tom Bradley remained calm. He was elaborately introduced to cheers and applause, and after it became quiet he leaned into the mike to say his first words as the leader of the city. He grinned, and with a twinkle in his eye, he diverted from his usual articulate delivery and said in the deepest voice, "Dis is da Mayor speaking!"

The windows in the pavilion almost shattered at the sound of the roar that followed. In five words he had reminded us of historical pain and gain.

He opened up the doors of city hall wider than they had ever been before. He set up a diverse selection committee for recommendations of people to the various city commissions. The appointments reflected the diversity of the city. Latinos became members of the Police Commission, Planning Commission and others, and he appointed the first Latino deputy mayor. He took the coalition of African Americans, Latinos, Jews, Asians, and Anglos that swept him into office and had us work together. We understood we all had a stake in the future. City contracts were opened up to minority contractors for the first time. He did it without fanfare. Things just got done.

Bradley went on to serve twenty years with many milestones, including the 1984 Summer Olympics. Buildings have been named for him. It's a nice gesture, but buildings in the west eventually get knocked down or renamed. In Tom Bradley's case, it won't matter. He knew that we're all like waves in the ocean. No one wave can do much; it takes the constant pounding of every wave to change the face of a coastline. Some waves only have the goal of just reaching the shore. He believed you must have commitment also if you intend to change the shoreline. That's why he threw himself at the shore of intolerance and prejudice. The shoreline changed.

Maybe that's why nobody names waves like they do hurricanes. There are too many of us and we keep on coming regardless of the season. "Da Mayor" understood and gave direction. Thanks, Mayor.

That's the view from the pier.

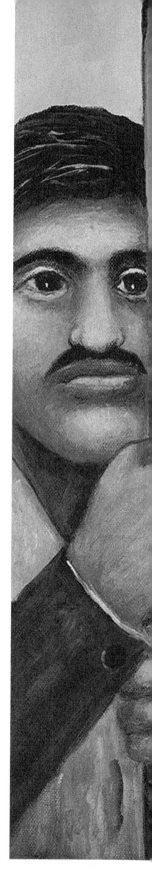

KATRINA

After Hurricane Katrina's destruction of New Orleans, blame is like my mother's beans at dinnertime. There's enough to go around for everyone. The only one who hasn't been faulted for Katrina's aftermath is God. I suspect we respect Mother Nature's whims. We've learned to deal with it.

If you live in the eastern part of the United States, you get used to snow and frozen winters. Reside in the South and be prepared for hurricanes. Tornadoes rip across the belly of our nation like a quick-spreading rash that leaves scars. Oceanfront dwellers recognize that their homes may become sea crab apartments. Mountain and forest folks fear fire and winds. Desert dwellers swell in the heat while praying for water. Riverside inhabitants expect floods. Dormant volcanoes don't always remain dormant. California contains more fault lines than the wrinkles on my forehead. The truth is that every inch of land in the United States is subject to earth-changing natural forces that humans can't control and in some instances can't even predict. We all live in harm's way. Some generated by ourselves.

John M. Barry's book, Rising Tide, describes the events and circumstances surrounding the 1927 Mississippi flood that left 700,000 persons without homes. Seventy-seven years later Katrina arrives. Its death toll is still unknown as of the date of this writing. What has evolved in those seventy-seven years is that we now expect government officials to protect us in times of great catastrophes. Our expectations are based upon the pronouncements that have come forth from officials with titles or candidates seeking them. When 9/11 occurred four years ago, we heard "never again." With fanfare, a national bureaucracy was established. It would coordinate rescue efforts. Free-flowing communication between teams bringing assistance to victims in time of disaster would be guaranteed.

Have some beans.

In both the 9/11 and the Katrina incidents, the media brought into our homes pictures of devastation as it was happening. Showing the hurricane, the screen images we saw contradicted the words we were hearing from those with titles. Even changing channels didn't make the screen support what we were being told by officials.

By the fourth day of promises, my co-passengers on Metrolink were ticked off and didn't care who was listening. They were embarrassed, felt betrayed and thought we looked like a third world country. Something else happened too.

The public image of lights, jazz and fun-loving New Orleans came crashing down. What was exposed were thousands of poor folks left abandoned to fend for themselves. A two-day warning to get out of town may be okay for rich and middle-class folks, but it is meaningless to those without transportation or the means to pay for it.

I'm not just picking on New Orleans, because if you take any city and rip off its publicized image, you'll find the poor. They live paycheck-to-paycheck or handout-to-handout.

We had a war on poverty in the sixties and have spent billions since then trying to eliminate poverty. It still remains, but in the shadows. Maybe eliminating poverty is not attainable by mankind. Race and sex discrimination were also attacked in the sixties. We had some success in that battle. At least there was racial and gender diversity in the decision-making this time (a black mayor, woman governor, and white males). Have some beans.

Federal law requires that in education no child will be left behind. Schools failing to comply get sanctions. How about requiring that in times of peril no one will be left behind? If any are, put the officials behind bars.

That's the view from the pier.

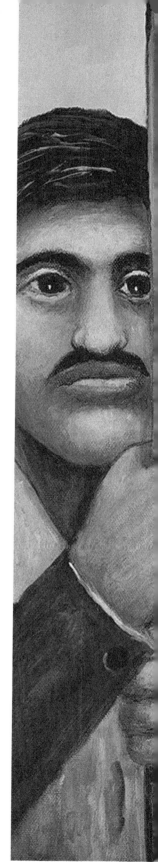

<u>MY VOTE</u>

As the smoke lifts from the recent election battlefield and the political analysts interpret the results, it becomes clear that my vote was really important this year. You see, I am a Democrat, married, Christian, Latino, senior citizen, middle-class lawyer now residing in San Clemente and working in Los Angeles. Political power brokers are using my vote to enhance their position and political muscle.

Latino politicians point to the fact that I voted (I've been doing it for sixty years). They argue that my vote is part of an emerging power that needs to be reckoned with in California. I used to be part of a sleeping giant. No one argues whether Latinos are sleeping anymore. Not since Governor Pete Wilson rang the Proposition 187 wake-up call and Latinos responded with thirteen Latino state legislators, a Latino speaker of the Assembly, and a Latina congresswoman in Orange County!

Latino leaders are pointing out how the Latino vote was the swing vote in California, Florida, Arizona, Texas, Colorado, New Mexico and New York for President Clinton's victory. Talk about clout! That's seven states my little old vote swung.

Then there is the senior citizen bloc. The brokers are saying my vote assures us aged citizens that Medicare and Social Security shouldn't be messed with in the future. If the President and Congress try to fool around again with either program, they will have to contend with us "grey jaguars." Modern medicine has extended our life expectancy and we know we can shorten elected officials' term expectancy.

The Christian advocates continue with their criticism of the lack of strong moral fiber in our leaders and society today. They point to my vote as part of the sword that will strike down immoral elected officials if they don't shape up. My vote has a certain halo quality as I listen to them.

Democrats are using my vote to point out how they made inroads into the conservative Republican stronghold of Orange County as they point to the Dornan/Sanchez race. Local Democrats argue that in the future they can get elected to office in Orange County with more money from the national party. It's okay with me as long as they don't ask me for some of it. There are better things to bet on than Democrats getting elected in Orange County.

A deeper and more detailed analysis will be made to determine the impact of my vote in the middle-class bloc. In this arena all kinds of persons are taking credit for my vote and explaining the significance of it. I'm not sure I really understood all the economic factors that impacted my voting decisions. Conserving our infrastructure and reducing taxes are conflicting concepts. I don't think I was consistent. I'll let the brokers sort it out and have them explain it to me later. No matter, middle-class citizens will still pay taxes.

My vote as a married man really carries a wallop. Not only does my vote count, but also it influences Cora, my wife. She takes my sample ballot and uses it as a guide in casting her vote. She votes the opposite.

There are always measures on the ballot dealing with lawyers. Either someone is trying to take away our clients or cut our fees. We very seldom get painted as good persons on the television commercials. Consequently, the election pundits always check how people voted on lawyer issues. I think the general public sees attorneys like fingernails. You need them to scratch, but you have to keep them clean and, if they get too long, clip them.

Finally, there is my vote as a male. It will be measured against the women's vote and future candidates will try to make something out of the difference. They then will make appeals to me through methods advised by their consultants for future elections. Of course they won't know that my wife and four daughters have greater influence on my vote.

It's amazing how an X on a piece of paper can generate so many boasters and credit-takers. I've never met any of them. Nevertheless, it does feel good to know that I had such an influence on the outcome of the recent election. I can hardly wait for the next one. Who knows? They may have a fisherman's voting bloc next time around. Now, we're getting somewhere, even though it does sound fishy.

That's the view from the pier.

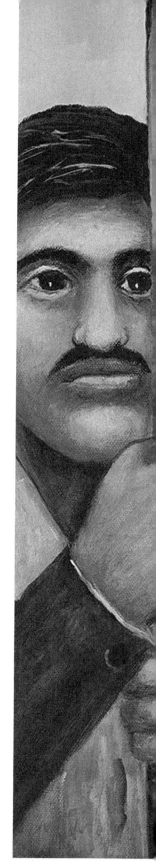

PAST AND FUTURE

Last weekend, the past met the future. The day before I was to attend a luncheon celebrating Justice Carlos Moreno's appointment to the California Supreme Court, I received a phone call. It came from an old-time client, teacher Sal Castro. Judge Moreno had been one of Sal's students.

Sal Castro had received notoriety in 1968 when he led four thousand East Los Angeles Chicano high school students in a walkout, protesting the quality of education. When the grand jury indicted him over the incident, I became his lawyer. Later, the court quashed the charges when it ruled they violated free speech.

Now, Sal wanted me to deliver a package to the judge. I did, and a big grin crossed Judge Moreno's face. The package contained a photo of a young Sal Castro as a coach, standing with his inner city Little League team sporting baseball caps and gloves. A small, young Chuckie Moreno knelt in the front row, pondering. I asked the judge when he knew he wouldn't make it as a professional ballplayer? He said sometime in junior high school. We laughed. Yeah, dreams change.

Later, Cora and I drove to Bakersfield. We were attending the seventeenth annual business conference at California State University Bakersfield. Nine thousand would attend to hear world and business leaders.

Security officers checked each of us as we entered the conference. A new addition for new times. After all, former U.S. President Gerald Ford, ex-President Ernesto Zedillo of Mexico, ex-Premier Ehud Barak of Israel and ex-Prime Minister John Major of England were the scheduled speakers. This was the fourth time we have attended, but never have I seen such an outpouring of love for country. Talk about patriotism! It filled the massive tent and spilled out onto the grounds. Speaker after speaker, Americans and non-Americans, praised our country and its love of freedom.

Throughout the day, my eyes swelled with tears and emotion blocked my throat. The September 11th terrorist attack erased all differences that people thought existed between them. Even James Carville and Bill O'Reilly, scheduled to debate, had difficulty finding a debatable issue. The terrorists' blow has bound us with a common goal: get the perpetrators and protect our way of life.

After we returned home Sunday afternoon, I sauntered out to the pier with fishing poles in hand. My son, Phil, and grandson, Andre, joined me. As we kept an eye on our rods and watched the surfers meet the challenge of the waves, I thought of the two gatherings.

I recalled Judge Moreno's reaction to the photo. He obviously had fond memories of his younger days under the tutelage of Sal Castro. The teacher's phone call to me evidenced the pride he felt over a former young baseball player and his student's success. It validated Sal's dedication to bettering the lives of inner-city children and fighting for equal education.

Then I thought of the speeches and solidarity I heard and witnessed in Bakersfield. The appointment of a former inner city Little Leaguer to the California Supreme Court added credibility to the conference's message. It also validated the words of encouragement that teachers like Sal give their students. This is how a democracy is supposed to work. Dreams are welcomed and encouraged to become reality.

I watched my son and grandson as they talked and took in the scene, one enjoying and pursuing his career in music, the younger examining his dreams. It doesn't matter which one Andre chooses. His country and father will let him pursue it. A young Chuckie Moreno hung up his little, old, tattered, leather baseball glove and dream of playing professional baseball to eventually pursue another career. Now he will sit on the high court of this state. I'm not sure who is more excited, Sal Castro or Carlos Moreno? It doesn't matter. California will always benefit from good relationships between a teacher and students.

That's the view from the pier.

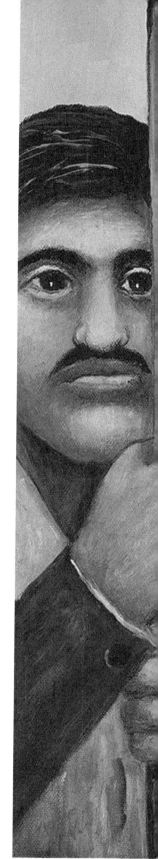

LEAP YEAR

The earth has a scheduled orbit around the sun. In the scheme of things this is not a big deal. After all it is just another planet staying in its orbit and not colliding with anything else in space. But since earth has humans living on it, our inquisitive nature noticed other heavenly bodies in the sky. We named them and discovered that their location consistencies served navigators well. It took us awhile to figure out that the earth wasn't flat. We also noticed the four seasons and kept track of their arrivals. That concept and knowledge led to creating calendars. But different cultures came up with different calendars.

Julius Cesar in 45 BC is alleged to have created a calendar with a leap year. Prior to that the calendar was a mess. In those days the last month of the year was February and the 24th day was followed by five days of feasting till the end of the year. But every four years the 24th day was made a 48-hour day and then the five days of feasting followed.

In 1582 Pope Gregory XII invented the Gregorian Calendar. December became the last month of the year with its 31 days. This new lineup brought the calendar closer to coincide with the time that the earth actually travels around the sun. The earth takes 365.24219 days to complete its loop, but our regular calendar only has 365 days. So what happens to the .24219 left over from each year? Not to worry. Every four years we tack on an extra day in February and that year becomes a leap year. Persons born on February 29 are called "leapings" or a "leaper."

During a regular year these folks celebrate their birthdays on February 28 or on March 1. I know none that forego a birthday celebration just because February 29 is not on the calendar. Leap years have produced various traditions in different countries. In the British Isles women were allowed to propose marriage only on leap years. In Denmark, refusing a woman's proposal, required the man to buy her 12 pairs of gloves. In Finland a man's refusal cost him fabric for a skirt. In Greece a marriage in a leap year was considered unlucky.

So what happens when February 29 falls on a work day? If you are on a monthly salary, you work an extra day without extra pay! They slipped that one in without fanfare. If I was on a straight salary, I wouldn't work that day. It's not my fault they can't make a calendar that doesn't know what to do with .24219 of a day. What about having a holiday every four years?

Look. In an election year, candidates seek votes from every identifiable group. The poor are promised money. The middle-class are promised stability. The wealthy are promised no taxes. Students are promised lower tuition. Senior citizens are promised longer life. What about the "leapings?" Out of every million persons 684 are born on leap year day. Why not promise everyone who works on a monthly basis a holiday on the 29th of February? Better for them to get the day off than let the employer get an extra day of work without having to pay for it. Those who work on an hourly basis might not mind getting a day off even if it means they don't get paid. Besides, think of the 684 persons out of a million who are born on the 29th of February. Who wouldn't vote for a candidate who declared a national holiday on his or her birthday? In a close election the "leapings" vote could be the difference between victory and defeat. Since presidential elections come on leap years, I don't know why the candidates never figured this out? That's the view from the pier.

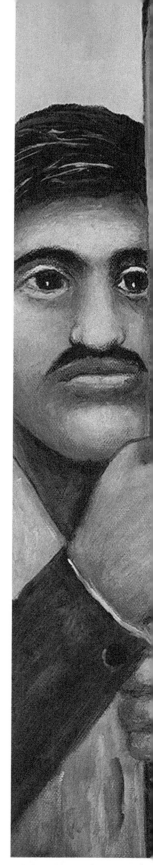

MEDAL OF HONOR

This year, President Obama awarded twenty-four Medals of Honors to veterans from WW II, Korean War and the Vietnam War. They had engaged in "personal acts of valor above and beyond the call of duty." That's the criterion for the award.

The concept of giving medals to military personnel in this country started with George Washington when he presented the Fidelity Medallion to three New York militia men. In 1782 he established the Badge of Military Merit in recognition of members of the Continental Army who performed singular meritorious action. In 1863, during the Civil War, Congress established the Medal of Honor as a decoration to be awarded military personnel. Initially, the award was limited to the Army, but subsequently all armed services were included. Approximately 3,468 Medals of Honors have been awarded. More than one-half of them were presented for action in the Civil War.

The nomination process requires the request to come through the military chain of command. For a while, another source for nominations came from Congressional members and special acts of Congress. But in 1917, an Army Medal of Honor Review Board struck 911 names from the honor roll for lack of basic prerequisites. It was important that only those who qualified should be honored. But were some excluded because of their race, ethnicity, or religion? In 1993 the US Army commissioned a review of war records and the commission found that African Americans had been excluded because of their race. As a result, ten African Americans were awarded the Medal of Honor.

In 1998 President Clinton awarded twenty-two medals to Asian Americans, including Senator Daniel Inouye. They too had been discriminated because of their ethnicity. Later, President Bush awarded Tibor Ruben the Medal of Honor, after a finding that he had been excluded because he was a Jew.

Then in 2002 Congress ordered a review of thousands of war records to determine whether Latino and Jewish veterans were denied the Medal of Honor because of their ethnicity or religion. The answer was yes. President Obama, at the White House presentation stated to the new twenty-four recipients, "No nation is perfect. But here in America, we confront our imperfections . . . . including the truth that some of our soldiers fought and died for a country that did not always see them as equal."

Among the recipients were Vietnam veterans, seventy-six-year-old Jose Rodela and sixty-eight year-old Santiago Jesse Erevia, both from San Antonio. It was a special day for Vietnam veteran John MacFarland. In 1969 he had recommended Erevia for the Metal of Honor and couldn't believe that Erevia hadn't received it. MacFarland was haunted by the thought that he hadn't been descriptive enough and continually inquired. Now he knows the reason for the delay. Family members of posthumous honorees joined the President as well. Some were not Latino nor Jewish. They were Distinguished Service Cross recipients who should have been Medal of Honor awardees.

Aside from receiving the Medal of Honor and being named in the Medal of Honor Roll Book, the honorees receive (1) a monthly pension above and beyond any military pensions or other benefits and cost of living increases, (2) their children are eligible for admission to US military academies without regard to the nominations and quota requirements (3) ten percent increase in retirement pay, and (4) invitations to all future Presidential inaugurations and balls.

Only one woman, Mary Edwards Walker, a civilian Army Surgeon has been awarded the Medal of Honor. What about the other women that have served our country? Will undocumented military personnel be discriminated against because they are here without papers? I look forward to the day when we no longer have a reason to apologize, because we learned to treat everyone equal. That's the View from the Pier.

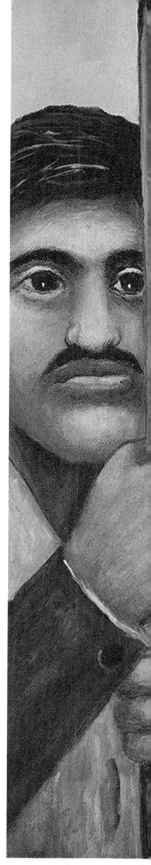

How To Improve Your Inner Artist.

Gain Recognition & Prestige by Becoming a Member of San Clemente Art Association.

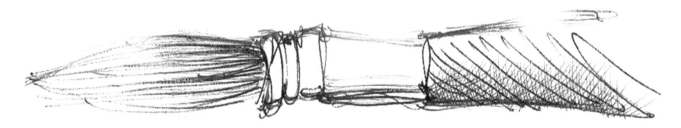

By joining the San Clemente Art Association, you will immediately start enjoying advantages that can further your art career. You will gain access to free instruction and workshop demonstrations from some of southern California's most prestigious artists. You will be invited to participate in monthly artist exhibitions that offer cash awards and allow you to exhibit in our updated gallery. You will be a part of an over 300 member organization of artists in every medium including painting, photography, jewelry and sculpture. We are a family dedicated to furthering the appreciation of Fine Art and Crafts and have been a part of the San Clemente culture for over 60 years!

For just $40. per year, you can start right away enjoying the benefits of membership and set your artistic career on a new path of growth and recognition. To sign up, just ask for a membership form at our Art Gallery, or download the form on our website at www.scartassociation.com. Do it today and start improving your inner artist right now!

San Clemente Art Association

San Clemente Gallery / Calle Seville & Avenida Del Mar / San Clemente, CA / 949-492-7175
www.scartassociation.com

PART FOUR: CHANGING TIMES

Over the course of the years change takes place. I have reflected on some of those changes while waiting for fish to bite.

Indian Chief—*I wanted to convey the Native Americans' loss over the course of history and their desire to retain a culture and identity.*

9/11

On September 11, 2001, I couldn't go to work. The high-rise building housing my law office was closed. Fear gripped Los Angeles. I wasn't sure what I felt as I watched the tragedy in New York unfold on television.

Was I watching a special effects movie? Were those real people leaping from flaming high-rise buildings? The huge dust mushroom from the collapse of the Twin Towers made me think of two outdated Las Vegas hotels meeting their man-determined fate.

I watched with numbness all day as commentators explained what we were seeing and our President advised us not to panic. Around four thirty I hit the pier, my place of solitude. A fishing pole accompanied me, more for ornament than anything else. I really wasn't out there to fish.

The sun dropped to the horizon, hurrying to put the infamous day to rest. My fishing line was in the water, but I hoped no fish would bite. I looked toward Dana Point and realized I had lived through four wars.

At seven years old, Pearl Harbor happened. I was afraid. The images of our sinking ships and the thought that someone didn't like America were upsetting. It shattered my world. By the time I was a high school senior, our nation was fighting in Korea. Then came Vietnam and the debate of whether we should be there. I was old enough and I thought smart enough to engage in the discussion. "Why are we there?" I asked.

Later in life, I visited Washington, D.C., and read the fallen warriors' names at their monument and cried for forgiveness. I prayed that never again would we send youth to risk their lives. The short Gulf War came next. We watched it on television. Our troops returned triumphantly with nary a scratch.

Now this. What is it? A war? A nightmare? Who's the enemy? What hatred the assailants must have had toward our country to convince them to die in suicidal missions. I tried sorting it out on the pier. Normally it blocks all land problems from the mind. Not on this day. The events were too devastating, too historical and unbelievable.

I watched the few strollers, a young couple with a child, maybe two or three years old. She giggled as she chased a pigeon. It flew away. An elderly couple sauntered by, holding hands, probably for the millionth time.

Then it hit me! What I was witnessing on the pier was freedom in its purest form, the liberty to walk without permission or approval. No armed guards. We trust each other. Strollers came knowing the pier was safe for body and mind.

That's what September 11 is all about. Someone is messing with our trust of each other. Democracy is built on it.

Law enforcement has identified the culprits and the investigation continues. Eventually, it will name those among the living responsible for those horrendous acts. Our leaders will determine our next steps, depending on where we are in the healing process.

We're victims and there are healing steps we must take as a nation. At the end we will survive and continue to live. Our challenge will be to decide how we want to live. That will be the debate and legacy for our children. How much freedom will we yield for guaranteed safety? Can it be guaranteed? No. That's democracy's risk and what makes it such a great experiment. Today it faces its most serious threat. The attackers took down buildings and killed thousands but didn't destroy our soul. Sure terrorists tried, but they underestimated our resolve. Our history shows we've paid dearly for freedom. Now, the cost just went up.

In the future, will little girls get to chase pigeons while old lovers stroll? Bet on it!

That's the view from the pier.

MISSING MEN

What happened to all the men? You know who I mean, folks like the "ragman," "junkman," "iceman," "bread man" and "ice cream man." They were around in my youth and I miss them. But I don't know when they disappeared. I just know that at some point they were gone.

My first memories of them were when we lived in a duplex on 53rd Street in southeast Los Angeles. A lot of men visited it. Hold on. Don't get the wrong idea! I'm talking about the iceman that came on a regular basis carrying a large block of ice that rested on a leather piece on his shoulder. The ice was held with big tongs. The iceman seemed huge and strong as he placed the ice in our icebox. As I think back now, he always got a cold shoulder.

The second man that visited our duplex was the milkman. I never saw him. I just know he came early and left milk on the porch and sometimes other dairy products.

The man I loved to see of course was the "Good Humor Man." He would drive slowly by in the afternoon playing a tune over loud speakers to appeal to every child. Upon hearing his tunes I would run to my mother crying, "Can I have an ice cream, Mama?" She came up with reasons why I couldn't. I think the mothers on our street had a pact because none of them purchased ice cream for their children unless the other mothers did too. The ice cream man probably caused more children to cry than any man in history.

An alley ran along the back of our duplex. I would run to the back fence and peer through it to see the junkman and his big horse, which pulled a wagon. The junkman's arrival was preceded by his loud voice yelling, "Juuunk maan, Juuunk maan." He took everything given to him. I know we never gave him anything because my folks didn't have anything to give anybody. Still there were those in the neighborhood who stopped him to unload unwanted and unusable items. I don't recall what he looked like; I just remember his big voice announcing his title and function. The same alley also served the ragman. He informed us of his presence by shouting in a songful manner, "Raaaaags. Raaaaags."

We moved to the first house my folks bought when I was eleven. It was on 73rd Street and had an alley also. But I never saw the ragman and junkman again.

The new neighborhood had different men. There was the bread man. He came in the afternoon in a Helm's truck with fresh breads and pastries. You could even order a birthday cake from him. His arrival came with a whistle and the housewives congregated around his paneled truck for bread and gossip.

The other man that came by our street was Tony, the vegetable man, ringing a large bell. He had a big black mustache and a beautiful Italian accent. Conversation with his women customers about fruits and vegetables delighted him. He would let them know what was in season or if there were shortages. They would squabble about price and quality, but he enjoyed it. "You want dollar products for penny prices. How I going to live?" he'd ask.

Eventually Tony and the rest of the men were not able to make a living delivering the services they provided. Modern technology and changing lifestyles eliminated their presence, just as automated elevators have eliminated elevator operators.

Today there are still men and women who provide services on a regular basis. The most common are gardeners. Maybe they will be able to withstand the change of times, since it is arguable that we will always want to see flowers and green lawns. I hope that will be the case. I'm not sure that's true for paperboys and mailmen. They are vulnerable to the same fate as Tony and the other men I remember. The arrival of the computer, e-mail, and the Internet present a faster method of delivery of information. Mailboxes may become items for antique collectors. As a new generation weaned on computers steps forward there will be changes.

I'm not complaining. Every generation will sometime in its evolution ask, "What ever happened to . . . ?"

The answer is, "They're gone."

That's the view from the pier.

CANCELLING CANCER

In December 2003, I took my annual physical exam. After further tests I was advised I had prostate cancer. What? The big C! Were they kidding me?

Fear froze my heart. The future became a lost concept. The prostate? What the heck was that? What did it do? The darn thing had cancer and I barely knew where the little bag was located. Cancer killed my mother and a brother-in-law. Now it was messing with me.

I met specialists. At seventy I had two options. I could do nothing and probably die of something else. Or I could treat the cancer. No-brainer for me. Where do I sign to get some action?

Now I had three options. One, I could have an operation to remove the cancerous little sack. I'd be off work for about a month, but the prostate and cancer would be gone. Two, I could undergo a five-day weekly external radiation treatment for eight straight weeks. Third, I could have radiation seeds implanted in my prostate. The implantation required a minor procedure and rest for a couple of weeks. Afterwards, I'd have a lap full of radiation for about six months.

Family and friends gave advice and I read a lot. To make matters worse, doctors couldn't agree if the cancer was confined in the prostate. Two said they believed it was; two said there was a possibility cancer was also outside the prostate's walls. Neither group was absolutely certain. Great.

I ruled out the operation, too intrusive and if the cancer was outside the prostate I'd still have to deal with it. The seed implantation only attacks cancer cells inside the prostate walls. External radiation covered the whole area. What to do? I opted for a combination, five weeks of external radiation and then implantation.

In May, I commenced daily at 7:00 a.m. for treatments at the Meiklejohn Radiation Oncology Center. Every morning radiation therapists zapped me with radiation I couldn't see. I lay perfectly still on a table and heard "zzzzzzzz" after they left the room. I never felt nor saw a thing. I believed the therapists when they said they were whipping that killer in my body.

After each session I caught my train into L.A. for work. I began wondering if this radiation process was a scam or was it really doing something?

As weeks passed, I accused the therapists of doing nothing but standing behind a door and making bee sounds. "How do I know you do anything?" I asked. "I don't see or feel anything. What happened to the old axiom, 'no pain no gain'?" They laughed and said they treat forty patients a day. That's a lot of folks with cancer.

After five weeks my body began to tire. Funny, I felt elated. Something was happening. The doctors nixed implantation. My pelvis was too small. So I stayed with external radiation treatments. July 22, 2004 was my last day.

That's when I decided to write this column. Readers should know that cancer isn't the end of life. It starts a new way to live. We men don't pay attention to our bodies growing up. Women watch their torsos more so. I suspect males would too if we gave birth. Yet, most men will get prostate cancer if they live long enough. At one time, finding a cancer survivor was as difficult as meeting a veteran kamikaze pilot. Today thousands of cancer survivors walk the earth. I've joined their ranks. The key to survival is catching the disease early. If cancer strikes, keep a sense of humor, pray and get guys like my therapists. Sure, your body may get tired from the radiation bombardment, but you're still alive. Besides, radiation made me a better fisherman. My bait glows.

That's the view from the pier.

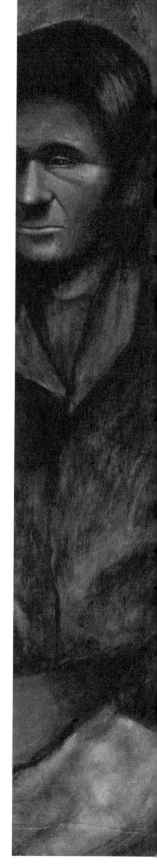

SHIRT TO DIRT

I opened the door to the broom closet and saw my old t-shirt hanging on a nail. It hadn't been there before. When new, this t-shirt had been my favorite because of its broad, horizontal, alternating bands of green and dark blue. I received it as a gift and we connected like salsa and chips; I wore it everywhere.

It was especially appropriate for beach living because of its nautical colors, loose fit, short sleeves and no collar. I felt like a sailor or someone who knew something about the sea when I wore it. Unfortunately, green and blue fade with each wash, and because the gift was worn so often it visited soap and water weekly. Fading colors eventually caused Cora to say, "You can't wear that to the restaurant."

Once I couldn't wear my t-shirt to nice places, my favorite upper body covering was grounded to home use only. We still managed to go occasionally to outdoor family gatherings. Cora reluctantly tolerated it. We didn't need to impress family.

Eventually, I had to admit that the tiny holes that began to appear erased the garment's use, even for family backyard barbecues. The shirt was really grounded now and I only wore it in the house, during "lay-back time."

One morning, I was running late to get to Dana Point for a fishing trip and quickly grabbed my old t-shirt, hurrying off with it on my back. We made it to the boat before it took off and I had one of the best fishing days ever. The grounded old shirt became my "new" lucky fishing buddy. We really had a relationship going. Thereafter, I never went fishing without my trusted and tested vesture. It had new life! Besides, scroungy clothes are in style on fishing boats.

Fishing clothes collect stains that the strongest detergent won't remove. These spots become reminders, medals of past fishing adventures and fodder for fish tales. Each wash tries to erase the stains but without success. It only diminishes color, thins the fabric, weakens threads, creates new holes and expands existing ones.

At some point, Cora must have held my old t-shirt up to the light and decided that the frayed neck opening and sleeves, along with the multiplying holes throughout, didn't allow the shirt to remain in the fishing clothes category any longer. She demoted it without due process and without telling me. My old, faded, green and blue covering became a dust rag. That's why it went from my dresser drawer to a nail in our broom closet. I'm not sure how long it had been there before I discovered it. Hopefully, just a short time.

A dust rag is one step above a plain "old rag." I shudder at using the term to describe my prized habit. After being an old rag only the trash can remains.

Upon seeing the new resting spot of my old t-shirt, I asked Cora to take it easy with her new dust rag and use it only on smooth surfaces. I knew it was useless to appeal her decision and plead for a life sentence as a fishing shirt. The case was closed. At this stage, I only want to prolong the cloth's life. It's been good to me and deserves a rest.

I wondered why I had these feelings about an old shirt? There had been a real tinge of sadness when I saw it hanging alone on a nail. Sure, there were the fond memories that I've mentioned and also the fact that the broom closet quarters represented the passage of time that could never return. But there was something much deeper that caused me sadness. It was the realization that we go through similar stages.

At some point we become faded and worn out. We don't go out that much anymore and limit ourselves to family functions. Some of us get a dye job, but inside we know we're not the same bright sparkling person on the outside that we were once. Lives get prolonged if we get new interests, as did my t-shirt when we became fishing amigos.

I figure I'm nearing the fishing clothes stage in my life. I hope that when I move on and become a dust rag, there will only be smooth surfaces.

That's the view from the pier.

AMERICA'S FACE

Ever wonder what an American looks like? Maybe as an artist I worry about that too much. But in the middle sixties a lot of Americans were going through an identity crisis. African Americans were shouting that they were "Black." Mexican Americans were shouting they were "Brown," while women were announcing at the top of their high pitched voices that they were "Woman."

I dealt with my identity issue by painting what I called the "Mexican American." My painting reflected two cultures. The American culture featured promptness and timeliness; the Mexican culture could care less. Other conflicting values emerged as I continued exploring my heritage. Upon completing my painting I realized I had two cultures swirling around in me.

See, Hernan Cortez invaded Mexico in 1519. He was a bearded Spaniard, and arrived at a country filled with brown skinned natives. By 1840, Mestizos were the majority of Mexico's population. The Indian and Spaniard intermarriages had created the modern Mexican. Today, we all have a picture in mind when a person is referred to as "Mexican." We artists paint those faces all the time.

Then a hundred years after Cortez landed, white-faced pilgrims came to Plymouth Rock. The descendants of those pilgrims became the faces of our founding fathers and ultimately the accepted white face of Americans. Sure, other colored faces existed and were American too, like the black, brown and lighter brown faces. But if you were an artist those faces didn't count if you were painting America's portrait. The accepted face was a white European looking person.

But things have changed. The census bureau recently reported that children born to Latino, Asian, African Americans and mixed-race parents now constituted a majority of all births in the United States. This happened in California three decades ago. If it were not for minority groups' births, the U.S. population would have been on decline. Four states already have a population where non Hispanic whites are in the minority, Hawaii (22.9%), California (39.7%), News Mexico (40.2%) and Texas (44.8%).

Today, the elected representative face of America is that of an African American, President Obama. Would a painting of an African American face other than President Obama's be received as the portrait of an American? Maybe, maybe not. I believe America is in the process of defining what an American should look like. Some folks don't want to let go of the old image.

But if you have watched the Olympic Games, you noticed that members of the United States teams have different colored faces and features. As a matter of fact, not all Asian looking faces belong to Asian countries. Different type faces are getting mixed in with other countries. Our world's population is literally being mixed before our eyes.

American artists have new types of faces to paint. Will one type of face emerge as the universally recognized face for the United States? Not in my life time. But that is our challenge. Artists must capture those qualities that define Americans. Our sense of independence, commitment to freedom, and courage to speak out, is our identity. Artists will be forced to portray those qualities in their portraits to capture the image of an American. The old method of skin color alone won't do it anymore. We are a more complex nation now. That's the view from the pier.

LAGOON BLUE

I noticed a new and different face. She looked like she came right out of a MTV music video. I stood along with the rest of the regular commuters at L.A.'s Union Station waiting for the doors to open so we could board the train. The crowd size grew. Each new arrival glanced at her, and then when she didn't notice, stared at her.

She wasn't the usual conservative white-collar worker waiting to head back to Orange County on the 5:37 p.m. Metrolink train. This was a teenager alone. Her hair was the grabber. It was cropped short all around, like a boy's, except for the top where it stood pasted straight up to form a thin four-inch-tall mohawk that ran down the middle of her head to the back of her neck. She had bangs that looked pasted on her forehead. The hair was a bright yellow except for the bangs and mohawk. They were colored blue.

Tightly around her neck was a two-inch-wide black leather band with chrome spikes and a loosely-fitted, big link silver chain held together by a brass lock. Around her waist were chain belts with locks and things hanging from them. Even her black tennis shoes had little chains and locks interwoven into white shoelaces.

She wore a sleeveless top made from a leopard skin-type design cloth. On the upper right arm were black letters in ink. Some letters also appeared on her fingers. I hoped the poor man's tattoos would wash off if and when she ever changed her mind.

A small, tight black skirt ended in the middle of her thighs. The tops of her black stockings reached two inches short of the hem of the skirt and were held by garter belt clasps.

The train's doors finally opened and I went to my usual place. She faced me in the same car but from another cluster of seats. A riding deputy sheriff took a double take when he passed her.

I studied her face. It had a tiny silver ring in one nostril and her blue eyes were lined with heavy black mascara. I looked through the makeup; she was just a girl. I thought of my four daughters.

Our car thinned out after each stop. No one spoke to her; they only looked. She didn't care. After the stop in San Juan Capistrano only she and I remained in our car. The next stop was mine.

"Going all the way to Oceanside?" I asked

"I'm going to San Diego," she answered, surprised that I had asked.

"There's an Amtrak that goes to San Diego."

"I didn't have enough money to take it."

"That's a good enough reason not to take Amtrak," I laughed and she now smiled.

"How are you getting to San Diego?"

"I don't know."

"What's in San Diego?"

"My boyfriend."

"Can't he pick you up?"

"He doesn't have a car."

"What are you doing with a boyfriend that doesn't have a car?" I joked. She didn't know how to answer.

"How long will the color in your hair last?"

"About two weeks."

"What do they call the blue?"

"Lagoon Blue."

"That's cool," I said in an effort to connect. She was like a little waif as she appeared to shrink before my eyes and smiled. She said her trip cost $9.50. Unnoticed by her, I had checked my wallet. I had a few bucks. As I got ready to leave, I handed her ten. "Get to San

Diego." Surprised, she smiled and thanked me. We talked briefly. She said her father died two weeks ago. My stop came and I had to get off; I had no time to hear or say more. The train pulled away with her in it.

What was she going to do? I should have given more. I wish I had more. What pulled me into a conversation with her in the first place? Was it because I saw her as a lost child? Did she symbolize the next generation?

She didn't know how she was going to get to San Diego but took a leap of faith . . . or desperation. Will her boyfriend ever appreciate what she did? Will he care?

Wearing Lagoon Blue was a bold statement of independence. Eventually the color disappears but not the underlying character of determination that caused her to use it. She should have that trait for life. I pray she'll know that and use it wisely.

That's the view from the pier.

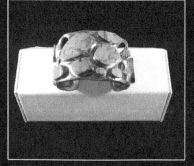

PART FIVE: FAMILY

Much of my time is spent with family. Mexican tradition requires this to be the case, but the truth of the matter is that I truly love and enjoy my family. What follows helps explain why.

Christmas Tamales—*Every Christmas our family gathers to make tamales that are eaten on Christmas Eve. This painting depicts our assembly line. The dog is my grandson Andre's dog, Banyan.*

TATITA

My sister, Elisa, handed it to me and said, "I think you ought to have this." I looked at the little black booklet. Its stiff cover had a seal and name on it, Operative Plasterers and Cement Finishers' International Association of the United States and Canada. The six-page log was my grandfather's union dues payment record from 1951 as a cement mason. He had been initiated into Local No. 627 on August 26, 1936, two years after I was born.

Fred Feliz, my grandfather, was a mystery man. He was tall, almost six feet, dark, strong, reserved and gentle with us grandchildren. We called him Tatita.

He couldn't read. His social security number was tattooed on his forearm. I remember him telling me that he was lead-man in charge of laying most of the cement sidewalks in Los Angeles. At the start of each job, he was given the plans and pretended to know how to read them. Then after his boss left, he stuck them in the back pocket of his white overalls. When an inspector or boss came, Tatita would pull out the plans. They'd check the work. Yep, everything measured out. Tatita said he learned his trade from doing it and knew how sidewalks were supposed to be and where they went.

He worked six days a week every day of his life, rising at four in the morning. On his birthdays, we had to be present before seven, because he was in bed at eight. On Sunday visits, I watched him clean and sharpen his tools in the garage. The work in the sun had made his face and hands a darker shade than the rest of his body.

I was around twenty-one when he fell ill. He had suffered sunstroke at work. After that, he was confined to his home. I'd stop and visit. We'd talk and he longed to return to work. I listened but had been told that he would never be able to go back. No one had told him. He spent hours in the garage sharpening his tools looking forward to the day he'd work again. At some point, Tatita realized he never would. After that, it seemed he shriveled up and died.

Last week, at San Juan Capistrano's train station, men were digging up the sidewalk and pouring cement to improve the boarding area. I watched them break up the old concrete, prepare the ground, lay the forms, mix and pour the cement, level and finish it. This work is for young men, too much back-bending for guys like me. I remembered the pride that Tatita had in the work he did. "People walk on my work," he'd say. His dues log came to mind. The last payment noted was in July of 1955: $2.50.

Last Saturday, at the pier rail, I thought of him and men of his generation. They never had moments like this, the time to do nothing. Then I remembered his hours in the garage. I smiled. Each man has a place where he can be somewhere else.

That's the view from the pier.

TWO TABLES

Family gatherings bring children and adults together. At mealtime, a significant question presents itself: separate table for the kids? At my grandmother's house the answer was yes.

So, we young ones were rounded up to eat by ourselves at a table, box or other flat-topped piece of furniture. Sometimes we had chairs; sometimes we sat on the floor. As a kid this arrangement seemed okay.

But when do you get to sit at the grown-ups' table?

In our family it took an act of Congress. It didn't matter that as a teenager I was taller than all my elders.

Only death of an existing occupant at the adult table or the purchase of a larger house would have put me with the adults. I didn't wish anyone's death and my grandparents weren't looking for a new house. So, I remained eating at the kids' table long after I graduated from high school.

On Thanksgiving, we gathered at my grandmother's for dinner. Nanita had a small dining room that only accommodated seven adults if they squeezed in. No room for me and my sisters, only space for the turkey.

As a young boy, a turkey leg represented power because Nanita made sure Tatita and my father each got one. Applause accompanied her placing the turkey leg plates before them. I thought the leg must be something special and dreamed of the day when I would earn the right to have one.

In my early twenties, Tatita passed away. At the next Thanksgiving gathering, I was invited to sit with the adults. Not only that, Nanita served me a turkey leg! My time had arrived. Savoring the moment, I took my first bite into the leg. I couldn't believe my taste buds. It was the worst piece of meat I had ever tasted—stringy, tough and dry.

"How do you like the leg, mijo?" Nanita asked. "Great," I lied. This was it? I waited all these years for this piece of meat and I had to finish it? It was a long meal. Nanita smiled as if she had given me a plate made in the king's kitchen. I wondered if she had ever tasted a turkey leg?

I never ate one again and still got to eat with adults. Once a member, always a member.

For all those minor years, I thought we sat at separate tables because of no space. Now I know the real reason. Cora and I supported the two-table policy. Parents got to enjoy a meal in peace with other adults. The tradition continues, but children grow up and bring grandchildren.

Now I hear my grandchildren's laughter and giggles at their table as their parents engage in discussions at our table. We discuss current events and tips on how to raise children. The first topic, I can do nothing about; the second one, I don't have a clue anymore.

I remember how I yearned to sit with the grownups. Now I make a point to drop by the grandchildren's table and tease them, so they know they're not forgotten. Maybe I'm better suited for the children's table anyway. Besides, I want to make sure the little darlings don't waste time savoring a turkey leg. Focus on the dessert.

That's the view from the pier.

CORA'S CHRISTMAS TREES

Christmas impacts everyone one way or another. Employers consider whether to pay employee bonuses and, if so, how much? Employees wrestle with whether to attend companies' Christmas parties.

Families plan and cook Christmas Eve and Christmas Day dinners. Parents and grandparents check bank accounts and credit card balances to see if they can match children's gifts expectations.

Church choirs rehearse carols and new songs. Preachers review their Christmas messages and pray that pews will be filled.

Dwellers decorate dwellings with lights that give evenings a special glow. Some displays draw crowds who marvel at the exhibits and wonder what they cost. Christmas light installers now provide a professional touch for the more affluent. The hills of San Clemente twinkle at night with blinking lights and Avenida Del Mar's trees sparkle with tiny white lights igniting excitement in the air. Government officials debate what constitutes acceptable Christmas displays in public buildings in order to avoid lawsuits over the issue of the separation of church and state. Non-Christian adults address questions from their children regarding the season and why other children get gifts and they don't.

Merchants, seeking a good year, display new merchandise in anticipation of an onslaught of eager buyers. Santa Claus visits malls and shopping centers to assure believers that he will visit every child on Christmas Eve. In spite of the technology available, old Saint Nick prefers to rely on his trusty reindeer to accomplish the feat. On foggy nights, he calls upon red-nosed Rudolph to lead the way. The old guy's effort to maintain consistency must be admired. He is so convincing that children leave their list and cookies for him before they retire to bed on Christmas Eve.

In preparing for his arrival, a Christmas tree is necessary. Picking one with Cora and the kids was always an adventure. She couldn't make up her mind as to which one to take home. Having five children and a docile husband at her disposal only compounded the problem at the tree lot. Whenever Cora thought a tree met her standards, she'd assign one of us to hold and guard it while she checked out other firs. This semi-ownership by possession kept other buyers at bay until Cora made up her mind. Before long, six trees were being clutched by a member of the Sillas clan throughout the tree lot. Cora walked back and forth between her stakeouts like the Commander-in-Chief inspecting forts. "Let go of that one," she'd say when she decided the tree in question wasn't really what she wanted. Then she'd pick another prospect that caught her fancy and assigned one of us to guard it while she continued her search for the perfect tree. Eventually, the tree contestants would be reduced to three finalists. By this time, two of us were watching each tree to make sure nobody would even think about taking them.

"What do you think, Herm?" she asked, as if it mattered what I thought.

"It looks okay to me," I'd answer. The kids were relieved as we carried the chosen tree to pay for it. We prayed that Cora wouldn't change her mind before we loaded the tree on the car. All that's behind me now since the kids moved out.

A few years ago, Cora purchased an artificial tree. I think she realized I couldn't guard all her nominees in the lot while she decided which one to take home.

Recently, from the end of the pier in the evening, I looked back to the twinkling shore lights. I thought back to those years when our children laughed and sang as we drove home Cora's winner. We knew we had the best tree ever to hover over the nativity scene.

How is it that a child born over 2000 years ago impacts us all now?

That's the view from the pier.

THE SECRET

What a weekend! Cora and I attended a blowout celebrating my cousin Aurora Gonzalez's fiftieth wedding anniversary. She and her husband, Momi, have seven children and those kids threw one heck of a shindig for their parents.

More than two hundred family members, friends and neighbors started filling the Gonzalezes' tent-covered backyard in Covina at 5:00 p.m. They kept coming. So did the music. First, came a trio. Within an hour, mariachis marched in with trumpets blaring to cheers. The mariachis and trio exchanged sets as new invitees arrived. Within a couple of hours, a band started setting up. It commenced when the trio and mariachis left.

The band's music was prom night stuff, slow and mellow with a hoarse saxophone leading the way. Talk about bringing back memories! Even Cora and I danced.

Heck, the whole night was one big memory bubble. Aurora's brother, Gilbert, came from Virginia with two of his sons. I reminisced with them as margaritas flowed and guests intermingled freely. More cousins arrived. Man, I hugged so many of them that when I woke up the next morning my arms stuck out in front of me like a U.

The catered food was quickly eaten as conversation and laughter filled the air. A short ceremony followed as Aurora and family stood next to the pool in front of an American flag. It had flown over the White House and their congressmen presented it to Aurora and Momi for this special occasion. The two aged lovers thanked their children. Brothers and sisters of the honored couple spoke emotionally as they bestowed congratulations and blessings.

I held back tears. After all, lawyers aren't supposed to cry in public. The gathering brought back fond memories of our parents, and how they instilled in us the importance of family. Here we were, their children with our children and grandchildren enjoying each other's company. I wandered from table to table talking to cousins and spouses, catching up with their lives and their offspring. Each little visit impressed on me the wisdom of our parents. They were probably looking down at us and congratulating themselves on their hard work as we continued to multiply and gather for these occasions.

I spoke with Momi. As a building contractor he still works daily and enjoys it. He started as a masonry apprentice and recalled his first job, working on a large stone for an architect-designed house. "One day this guy shows up on the job," Momi said. "Everybody is catering to him, so I ask my co-worker, 'Who is that guy?' He didn't know."

"The next day when I go back to work, there's this note on the stone, 'You masonry fellows are true artists.' It was signed, 'Frank Lloyd Wright.'"

"Wow!" I said, "Did you keep the note?"

"Nah. At the time, I didn't know who Frank Lloyd Wright was." We both laughed. Momi lamented how he never made a lot of money. To him the thrill was creating beauty, money was secondary.

I looked around at the love-packed, fun-filled party. His children and their spouses served as gracious hosts. The smiles radiated pride and love. I said, "Momi, you may not have made a lot of money, but you are a rich man."

He observed the scene, smiled, and nodded his head. I took a mental snapshot, because I knew when I'm out on the pier I'd sift through what I saw trying to learn the lessons of life. Fishermen do things like that when fish aren't biting

As we were leaving, I asked Aurora, "What's the secret to a fifty year marriage?" She smiled, then winked, "The bedroom, baby! The bedroom."

That's the view from the pier.

OUR OSCAR

In the early 1970s I served on an advisory committee to the United States Census Bureau. One of our duties was to advise the Bureau on how to count undocumented residents in the 1980 census. (Much depends on an accurate count, including the number of congressional members each state will receive.) Our committee recommended launching a campaign advising undocumented residents that being counted would be to their advantage. Their paper receipt would be evidence of their presence here in 1980. This fact could assist them in the future to become legal residents and citizens. The message worked. More undocumented residents had themselves counted in the 1980 census than ever before.

Later, Congress passed a new immigration law giving amnesty to persons who had been in the United States since 1980. This new law would affect me personally, although at the time I didn't know it. What I did know was that the new law required every employer to have proof that each employee was here legally.

Our law firm hired a receptionist. Get her papers I insisted. She gave different excuses for failing to provide them. Finally, she admitted she had illegally crossed the Canadian border. Our firm was the first employer to ever ask for her papers even though she had worked here for ten years. We let her go. So much for employers' sanctions. Even if she had produced documents, how were we to know if they were fake or not?

The INS constantly raided a client of ours who manufactured tortillas. His undocumented employees would return within a week. The INS agents never asked the client for his papers since he was the owner. If they had, he would have had to accompany his employees. That never happened.

Antonio—*One of my grandnephews.*

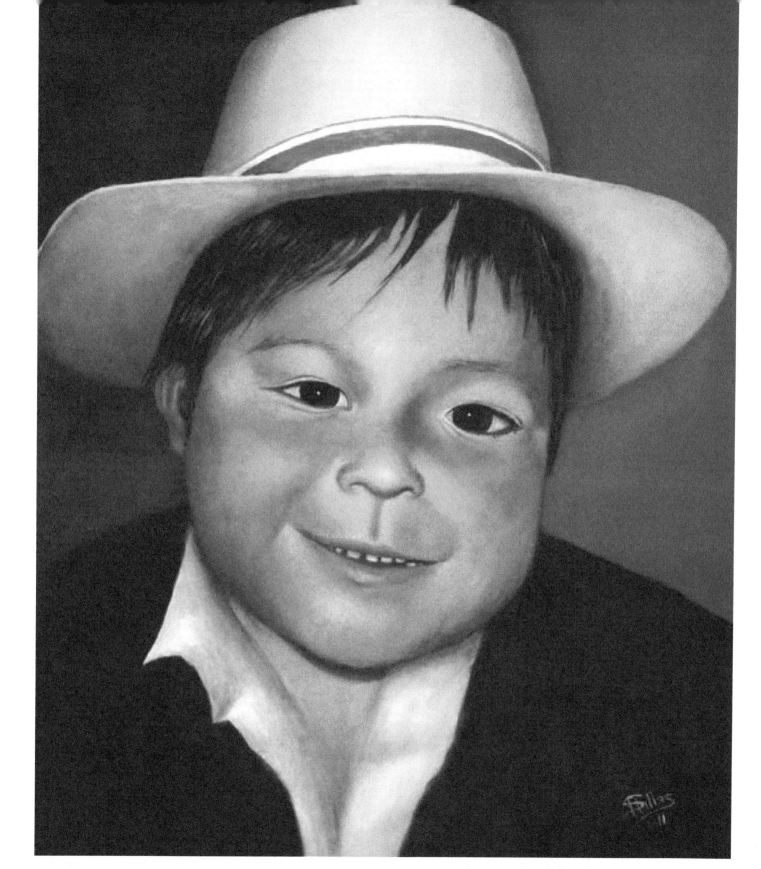

What did happen was that an El Salvadoran mother, Zaida, left her children and war-torn country in the 1970s to come to the States. It represented a safe haven where she could get a job and ultimately raise her children in a safe environment. She left her children with relatives. Zaida intended to bring her children across later. Years passed before she could do that. Finally her fourteen-year-old, Oscar, was informed his mother was ready for him in the United States. He had been harassed by the military and guerillas. Each wanted to give him a rifle to fight the other. Guerillas would enter his classroom with weapons drawn to recruit young supporters. Oscar fled at the request of his mother. He crossed our border on his second try into her awaiting arms. The young El Salvadoran now was able to go to school without having to see blown-up body parts lying along the route.

After entering college and joining UCLA's Mexican Folklorico dance group, he met Monica, our daughter, who also danced. They fell in love, married and have provided three fantastic grandchildren. Once during one of our many conversations, Oscar told me his mother got her papers after the amnesty in the 1980s. She had proof of their presence here because she had filled out the 1980 census form and kept a receipt. Love finds a way.

Today, Oscar teaches at the high school level. His young Latino students relate to him as he teaches them English and provides living proof that the United States is the land of opportunity. Recently, seven hundred students walked out of his school and joined thousands of other students demanding that a comprehensive immigration law be enacted that would prevent their parents from being uprooted and deported. Most parents work and some hold two jobs to make ends meet. They dream their children will become like Oscar in the future.

No one is sure how the Washington D.C. crowd will resolve the numerous issues facing our nation as it again wrestles with carving out an immigration policy. I'm glad we dealt with it in the 1980s. Our nation made the right decision then and our family received an Oscar, Oscar Vasquez.

That's the view from the pier.

Hogans
Bait & Tackle

Dana Point, CA

Full Service Tackle Store Including:
Poles, Reels, Hooks, Sinkers, Fishing
Lines, Equipment, Clothing, and
Fishing Information
Live Bait & Frozen Bait Available
Rod & Reel Repair

Open 7 days a week
8:00 A.M. to 6 P.M.
34320 Pacific Coast Highway, Ste G
Dana Point, CA 92629
949-493-3528

Part Six:
Among Anglers

When we arrived in San Clemente, I went to the pier to fish because my father had taken me fishing when I was a little boy. The idea that I could now walk to a pier and fish was unbelievable. Since that first day, twenty-five years have passed. During that time I have met a great group of anglers, both local and from afar. Many have become my friends and we share bait, stories, and time. The most precious thing we share is the love for fishing. The stories that follow may help you understand why.

Fishing at Dawn—*Dawn is my favorite time to fish. Here three men with visions of many fish get ready at dawn.*

93

FISHING BUDDIES

I've been fishing for a long time on the pier. Anglers have come and gone, but I'm still not alone. John Yamada has been fishing on Saturdays over the last twenty years. He comes with a granny cart loaded down with buckets, fishing tackle, poles, bait, newspaper, chair, net and food. He uses a cane now to get around, but fish don't know it. John still catches them.

He's a quiet fisherman at sunrise. John goes through the ritual of checking his gear, cutting up his bait and getting comfortable for the day. He places a small bell on the tip of each pole. It's his alarm system. We all know how John is doing from the sound of his bells. Yet, it's not the fish that bring him out from La Puente. It's something else.

I see Joe Awad, who comes from Ontario. He's been fishing here for about fifteen years. Originally from Lebanon, Joe and family came to the States in 1986. Lebanon was too dangerous. Joe sold everything including his fishing boat to get here. He never looked back. Joe loves this country.

"It's good," he says as he empties his granny cart filled with fishing gear.

I think of his fishing buddy, George Akawe. He's also from Lebanon. George loves fishing more than anyone I know. Sometimes he comes during the week. Joe and George call each other regularly and share fish reports. The reports might be exaggerated, but that's acceptable. Joe is often on the phone with George giving him an update on the fishing. Last week, George told Joe how many fish he caught.

Joe couldn't sleep all night thinking of fishing Saturday. It now costs him sixty bucks for gas to get here but there's never a question in his mind about taking the drive.

Most Saturdays, John brings Joe the bait he's asked John to get for him at the Seal Beach bait shop. John doesn't mind. They understand that they need to do what they do every Saturday. They each have tales of their biggest fish and the larger ones that got away.

But, it's not the fish that brings us out. We're here because we have to be. Something draws us to this place. Maybe it's the sea air freshness, or the solitude, or the waves, or not having to report the time we spend to a clock or to anyone. We enjoy the pier pals who walk the pier and tourists who inquire about our catches. We talk to each other about sports, maybe fish, but most of the time we're quiet, just listening to our thoughts. That's what fishermen do. We can't explain why.

As I left John and Joe on the pier and headed back home, I saw another familiar face, Pat Yoshida. He was unloading fishing gear from his truck. "Where's your dad?" I asked.

"He passed away, March 11," he said with a sigh.

"Oh, no," I said, feeling like I had lost a good friend. Pat's father, Jose, was seventy-eight years old. He would stand next to his pole looking out at the sea with his son by his side. Jose and I bought each other coffee and praised the action or cursed the inaction. "Man, did he love to fish," I remembered.

"Yeah, he did. We buried him with his pole. I'm out here today in his honor keeping the tradition going," Pat said, his voice fading.

I nodded and headed up the hill. Being buried with a pole is a nice touch, I thought. I'd want bait too, just in case. Then, the fisherman's prayer came to mind:

> I pray that I may live to fish until my dying day.
> And when it comes to my last cast,
> I do humbly pray,
> When in the Lord's great landing net and peacefully asleep,
> That in His mercy I be judged big enough to keep.

Jose was a keeper.

That's the view from the pier.

THE EIGHT-FOOTER

Whenever I went to the pier, I felt I had let my dad down. See, he had left me his three custom-made, sixty-year-old fishing poles. I had refurbished two, but the third rod, an eight-foot surf pole, remained in my garage.

According to a Dana Point craftsman, the pole was too far gone for a facelift. He said since the varnish had peeled off, the pole had dried out and it didn't make sense to spend money to fix it. He scolded me for letting the pole get to such a condition.

So every weekend, I saw my sin hanging on the garage wall as I headed out to the pier. Well, a couple of months ago, Ray Hedge was back. He used to be a pier regular. Then, he moved to Rockport, Texas, a couple of years ago. The old salt had a dry wit and I'd give him a bad time about his fishing ability or clothing. One thing he could do was fix poles. Ray had already restored one of my dad's rods.

As Ray and I traded stories upon his return, he mentioned he was taking some poles back with him to fix for the local anglers. Then I thought of my dad's eight-footer withering away in the garage. "Hey, Ray, would you take a look at an old pole and see if you can do anything with it?" I asked.

"Sure," he said.

The next day, I brought out dad's rod. Ray examined it carefully and stroked his chin. I watched the expression on his face waiting for a sign. Leaning the pole against the pier rail, he said he thought he could "fix her up." I wanted to hug the guy but restrained myself. So, he took the rod back to Texas.

A couple of weeks ago, Cora called me at the office, "Your pole arrived."

The train ride home that evening seemed longer than usual. I was still in my suit and tie as I wrestled with the taped-up tubed package to get it opened. Finally, my dad's eight-footer emerged. It was beautiful!

"They don't make poles like this anymore," I told Cora as I stroked the old oak handle with a rubber base. I bent the rod's tip pretending I had landed a big one. "I'm getting a new reel," I said as I caressed my dad's legacy.

So last Sunday, on Father's Day, I took the revived eight-footer with me out to the pier. My guilt was gone. I told everyone I was fishing with my dad. The old pole hooked up with six fishes! One was a keeper.

A lot of fathers were out there Sunday, many with sons. While I prepared to go in, a young father fishing with his five-year-old boy talked to me about bait. His son was holding a pole with great expectation. Then it hit me. The boy didn't have a clue about the bond that was being created between him, his father and the sea. This is how it starts and it lasts forever. I smiled, gripped my dad's pole, and said, "Let's head in, Dad."

That's the view from the pier.

OCEAN FESTIVAL

The San Clemente Ocean Festival was a humdinger. By 6:30 a.m., folks were occupying the beach and pier. Fishing buddy Manny Jeslva already had our spot, since he knew I was entering the fishing tournament.

As I approached him, I greeted three of the Morrone brothers: Carmen, Aldo, and Adam. Carmen tells great stories of the pier in the old days and of Italy.

George Akkaoui and his clan were already set up. He drives from Pasadena, bringing friends and relatives. They generally take home a bucket full. Another resident and weekend angler arrived but passed on the tournament.

I paid my five-dollar entry fee and received an orange wristband. Everyone said I looked like a hospital escapee. Some jokingly offered to give me their catches for the tournament. I declined but thanked them anyway.

Kenny Iwakoshi sauntered by with Nicholas, his five-year-old son. Both had orange wristbands. Nicholas has been fishing since he could say "Da Da."

Two colorful balloon archways hovered over the pier. The fish probably knew something was going on and weren't biting.

Music floated out from the shore while surfing and swimming contests commenced. Signs posted on the south rail of the pier-reserved spots for woodies that arrived at 9:30 a.m. As the classic cars slowly edged their way to their spots, the old pier moaned. The autos' owners, most of whom had grey hair or none, polished their motor treasures as spectators grew in numbers.

Got Him—*A moment that will last forever.*

Fishing on the south side of the pier was over. I still didn't have a decent fish. I said I was going to ask for a refund, but I remained hopeful as people poured out for the festival. It kicked into high gear. Slick, tanned bodies dove into waves to start a race that took them out beyond the pier's end. The Beach Boys' sounds, emanating from the woody behind me, drowned the music from shore speakers. Strollers' bodies of all colors, shapes and sizes responded to the beat.

Local kibitzer John Lichty sauntered out to tell us there were no fish out here. Who could argue? Don Owen passed by on his motor-driven fish cart heading farther out. Mona Eyman, a great woman angler, joined him. Brothers Bill and Wally Kahale were doing their best, as always. Nador Akkaoul, a frequent visitor, watched his line patiently.

The clouds finally left like unwanted relatives and the sun welcomed an arriving train. I still hadn't caught a contender. Folks spilled out onto the pier as anglers joked back and forth sharing tales. Finally, I landed a seventeen-inch croaker! I figured I had a shot as the tournament ended.

King Neptune arrived at noon to crown the winner. Five-year-old Nicholas whipped us all with his twenty-inch croaker. We told the judges the kid had brought the fish from home. Nicholas, smiling ear to ear, was not to be thwarted as he proudly gripped his prize, a new pole.

While I trudged up the hill pushing my cart, I realized we fishermen had spent the morning joking, telling stories, some true, but all the time laughing. Folks thought we came to fish. I knew better.

That's the view from the pier.

A FATHER'S DAY LESSON

With a fishing pole in hand I eagerly strolled out early to the pier on Father's Day. I intended to get a few hours of fishing before my clan hit town. Other men had the same idea. They came with a tackle box, a smile, a rod and a knowing nod.

We were all taking a recess from playing father. For the moment, we were on our own enjoying the freshness, beauty and solitude of the ocean. Yeah, it was a man's thing picking the spot, setting up, baiting the hook and casting lines out into the swells and waves.

The fish cooperated for a change and croakers began appearing on the planks. They were the ocean's gifts to us on our special day. It was about time.

I looked up and down the pier and saw peace in the eyes of the men. The troubles and worries of the week were gone. On the pier, problems don't last any longer than a piñata at a Mexican birthday party. Someone in our lives had taught us how to fish and the serenity that comes with it. I suspected most of us had learned from our fathers. Maybe we were unknowingly paying homage.

As the hours passed, the pier filled with more fishermen and strollers. I hooked up to a good-sized croaker. After I landed it, I turned and saw this fellow grinning. He said to his young son, "See, he caught a fish."

I smiled and couldn't help but notice that the man's arms and hands were much smaller than normal. His hands only came to his waist and appeared to be nonfunctional. I figured him to be a tourist out with his kid and continued fishing. The early sun gave notice of a beautiful day.

Around ten, I packed up to head home. I saw across the way the man who had commented about my fish earlier. He was fishing with his sons, but something was different. I watched as he tied a hook on his line, cut his bait and baited his hook with his toes

As he sat on the pier's boards, he slipped his left foot into a sandal strapped to the heavy end of his fishing rod. The toes on his right foot cinched the straps of the pole sandal onto his left foot. His right toes set his spool reel for casting and held his line. He swung his left foot strapped to the pole and cast out his line like an eager angler. Then he set the drag with his right toes and leaned the pole against the rail. He was set and had done all this without the least bit of hesitation or difficulty.

His ability amazed and impressed me. After I finished packing, I walked over and struck up a conversation. It turns out he is a San Clemente resident. He's thirty-seven and has been fishing since his father taught him as a young boy.

"What's the biggest fish you ever caught?" I asked.

"A thirty-pound bat ray."

"Wow! That must have been something."

He smiled and told me how he started out fresh water fishing but now sticks to salt water and has a boat, but it's presently out of commission. He wasn't. I marveled at his dexterity and determination to fish. He had learned more than just how to fish from his father. Now the two sons fishing had obviously been taught how to fish but they also were learning a great lesson in life.

In fact, their father was teaching all of us that morning. I don't know if he caught anything. It really doesn't matter. His sack is full already.

That's the view from the pier.

FISHING AND TATTOOS

Here in San Clemente, the Ocean Festival completed another successful weekend. For two days folks from Southern California come every year to participate in this festival. Surfing contests, fishing tournaments for children and adults, various races on land and sea, a collection of beautiful refurbished old "woodies" parked on the pier, and a sand castle contest are just some of the events that draw folks here. Music blares from the loud speaker on the beach to put everyone in the mood for a party. Artists and vendors set up under tents plying their wares and work for two days on the waterfront.

As I stood next to my two motionless fishing poles that lean on the pier's rail, I concluded that what makes this event successful are people. Some locals stay away, "Too crowded," they say. Others stay away because parking is a problem. Free bus rides to the pier from San Clemente High School's parking lot ends that issue. Meanwhile, Amtrak passengers from the north and south disembark at the foot of the pier. They make their way to see the contests and displays. Dress is casual. Men are in shorts or bathing suits with beach shirts or are bare-chested. Women, depending on their age, walk in bathing suits or loosely fitted wear revealing as much skin that they think is appropriate. Pier folks walk at a slow pace. The faster you walk the sooner you get to the end of the pier and have to turn around. That ends the time that you have your back facing the shore and your eyes focused on the horizon where the sky smoothly massages the sea.

As the people pass me, I notice the increase in the number of tattoos. At one time the only tattoos you saw on the beach were on bodies of sailors or marines. You also concluded that the artwork was a result of a wild night ashore. That is not the case anymore. Pieces of art appear on bodies of all colors, ages and gender. The size of the work can be from one inch to a piece that covers a whole torso, legs and arms. The subject matters are endless. Humans' imagination has no boundaries, nor does mine.

I wondered what I would do if someone offered me their body to tattoo an image. Then my mind began to think about the evolution and the theory that the human body has evolved from a form that was also the source of the ape. What if tattoos could bring about such a mutation so that the carrier's descendants would be the recipients of a gene that would carry tattoos on a human body? The method of putting tattoos on a body has changed from punctures in the skin by sharp natural objects to motor driven machines outfitted by a numerous needle set-up. Could not new tattooing methods bring about a mutation among us? It only takes one to start it.

Imagine if tattoos were to become part of our descendants' skin the same way that color is passed on to their bodies. Would future generations be able to select the colors or images they wanted their child to have and the area where an image is to appear? "That would not be fair to the child" you say. What input does a child have about its name? None. It's born and the name comes with it. What about a child born with its name already on its body?

"How could this happen?" you ask. I don't know, but since we had a common ancestor with an ape, anything is possible. That's the view from the pier.

BIG HAL

I met Big Hal at our family's first annual fishing derby, the day after Thanksgiving. The tournament started at eight thirty in the morning on the pier. It would last for three hours. I provided rods, reels, bait and instructions. In addition, I served as judge.

The clan sauntered out about nine. By nine thirty all contestants had lines in the water. They numbered about fifteen. Things were really slow. A few fish had been caught, measured and tossed back. Too small. I kept busy baiting hooks, passing on words of encouragement and listening to family gossip.

One pole remained unused, so I placed an old anchovy on a hook and dropped the line over the rail. I left the pole unattended as I roamed around urging everyone to start catching fish.

Suddenly, my daughter Monica said, "Dad, the tip of your pole is moving!"

I looked. "Oh, it's just the waves, babe," I said like an old salt but grabbed the pole anyway. I jerked it and had something on! My pole bent over as a fighting resident of the sea sought the bottom. The reel screamed as the monster peeled off line. All I could do was hold on to the pole and pray the big fish would tire.

Finally, I started reeling it up. I felt like I was pulling up a barn door. "Get the net!" I yelled.

By this time everyone was looking down over the rail. Then we saw it! A halibut! I'm talking BIG HALIBUT, about maybe forty pounds! Rory, one of my sons-in-law, quickly lowered the net down. The fish was longer than the diameter of the net.

Then the halibut decided to make a final thrust for freedom and dove to the bottom. He pulled line off my reel again and headed toward the pilings. If he got in there, I'd lose him.

So, trying to avoid that, I did a very amateurish thing, I put my thumb on the line. The twenty-pound-tested line wasn't strong enough and snapped. Everyone groaned. Big Hal had escaped.

For the rest of the day, everyone kidded me about how we could have had a fresh halibut instead of warmed-over turkey. From that point on, I was determined to meet Big Hal again but hopefully with a different outcome. For a year, when I fished on the pier, I baited one pole especially for him. He never came.

Then at last year's family fishing tournament, I assumed my usual role. We talked about Big Hal's past visit. When things slowed down, I threw a line into the water and thought of our encounter. I left the pole against the rail and walked over to help grandchildren. Time passed as I enjoyed the morning.

Suddenly, Monica yelled, "Dad, your pole!"

I turned around and faced where I left it. It was gone!

Monica pointed to the water. "Your pole bent and then went over the rail. Something really big must have taken it!" she said.

Big Hal? This time he took my pole and a reel! Now he's getting personal. I became more determined than ever to hook up with him again. Time passed. Then one day, one of the local fishermen was fishing on the pier. He told me how, the day before, he had hooked a monster halibut but lost him in the pilings. Big Hal is still hanging around, gloating.

Then one morning I was fishing with one of my favorite fishing buddies, Steve Carrico. We were near the lifeguard tower on the pier. I had a line in the water and saw the tip of my pole quiver. I immediately grabbed my pole and yanked it up to set the hook in the mouth of the fish. I started to reel in my catch when, all of a sudden, my pole was yanked out of my grasp by a powerful force that took my pole over the rail and into the water below.

"Holy cow," I yelled as I looked over the rail to see where my pole had gone. It had disappeared!

"If I hadn't seen it, I wouldn't believe it," Steve shouted as he looked bewildered.

"I had a fish on and then something came and took what I had on the line," I said as some form of an explanation.

"It must have been a monster," Steve said by this time laughing so hard he was bent

over.

Big Hal, I figured. The rest of the day I was kidded about losing a fishing pole right out of my hand. One fishing joker said that he saw a submarine periscope in the water, but then realized it was my pole. I was the story for the day.

We anglers are the ultimate optimists. I know I'll meet up with Big Hal again. He's become my Moby Dick. When we do, I'll be ready. Besides, he owes me two rods and reels plus a fish.

That's the view from the pier.

Our Savior's Lutheran Church and School

Inspired to Love
  Encouraged to Think
    Sent to Serve!

Worship that is refreshingly honest and engaging
  (Sunday: 830 am;1030 am and 6:00 pm)
National Blue Ribbon Elementary and Preschool

*Serving the
Surfing faithful
since 1953!*

www.oursaviorsonline.com 949.492/6164

HERMAN SILLAS

Herman Sillas is a native of Los Angeles, and when he was 12, his mother enrolled him in a neighborhood Saturday morning painting class. Three years later his art instructor referred Sillas to the renown Otis Art Institute. Two years later he was awarded a scholarship there. After graduating from high school, he put his art career on hold to attend UCLA's undergraduate and law school. He opened his Los Angeles law office in 1960. As a young Mexican American lawyer in the turbulent '60s, he represented young Chicano activists. His paintings reflected the frustration and anger of his clients. Sillas' involvement in the Chicano Movement led him to politics where he served as California's Director of the Department of Motor Vehicles under Governor Jerry Brown from 1975-

1978. He was subsequently appointed United States Attorney for the Eastern District of California by President Jimmy Carter and served in that capacity from 1978-1980.

Following his stint in government, Sillas returned to Los Angeles and private practice. Encouraged by Mexican muralist Armando Campero, Sillas began painting with new vigor. His work reflected his Mexican heritage and love for people. He also began writing. Sillas and his wife moved to San Clemente in 1988, after their five children had married and left home. It was here that he was introduced to the San Clemente pier. The openness and freedom he experienced on the pier motivated him to write a monthly column called "View from the Pier."

Today, he continues practicing law, explores through his art and writings, his cultural roots making use of an inquisitive mind, experienced eyes, a master's brush and pen using color and words that convey emotion. As an award winning artist, Sillas' art work has been described as "pictorial memories of a witness to social change." His writings convey more than that. He loves the pier and its gift of peacefulness. He doesn't view a pier as a boardwalk above the waves. In the mind of this old fisherman a pier is a pathway for inspiration to write what he sees and thinks. Both his art and writings may be seen at his website www.hermansillas.com. He may be reached at sillasla@aol.com

CPSIA information can be obtained
at www.ICGtesting.com
Printed in the USA
BVOW05s1538101117
499966BV00030B/1546/P